M000252136

LOGGED OFF

MY JOURNEY OF ESCAPING THE SOCIAL MEDIA WORLD

Signature

LOGGED OFF

MY JOURNEY OF ESCAPING THE SOCIAL MEDIA WORLD

JORDAN WELLS

Scott and Scholars Press
East Orange, New Jersey 07017

Scott and Scholars Press® is a registered trademark of
Jordan Wells Publishing.

Publisher's Cataloging-in-Publication Data

Names: Wells, Jordan, author.
Title: Logged off : my journey of escaping the social media world / by Jordan Wells.
Description: Includes bibliographical references. | East Orange, NJ: Jordan Wells, 2019.
Identifiers: LCCN: 2020900420 | ISBN: 978-1-7344322-0-6 (Hardcover)
Subjects: LCSH Wells, Jordan. | Internet addicts--Biography. | Internet addiction. | Internet--Psychological aspects. | Social media. | Cell phones--Social aspects. | Social media addiction. | Internet--Social aspects. | BISAC BIOGRAPHY & AUTOBIOGRAPHY / Personal Memoirs | COMPUTERS / Internet / Social Media COMPUTERS / Social Aspects | SELF-HELP / General | POETRY / GeneralClassification: LCC RC569.5.I54 .W45 2020| DDC 616.85/84/092--dc23

ISBN: 978-1-7344322-1-3 (Paperback)
978-1-7344322-3-7 (eBook)

First Edition 2019

Jacket design by Jordan Wells/in collaboration
With www.thelovinglion.com

For special inquiries, please email us at scottandscholarspress@yahoo.com

Printed in the United States of America

10 9 8 7 6 5 4 3 2 1

CONTENTS

I would like to dedicate this book to my beloved grandparents;

And my dear friend Nannette, who I miss very much so.

A Riddle for You

You like me more than anything on this earth,
yet you can only find me on social media.

What am I?

Introduction

So, where do I begin? I will start on August 25th, 2018. It was a quarter to five in the morning. I woke up with anxiety, the worst I have had in a long time. My heart and mind were racing. I was having a mental meltdown. I was even getting emotional about this whole situation. It felt like my brain was being untangled and used as a jump rope. I did not know what to do at that moment. So, I quickly got out of bed, headed down to my basement, and hopped on my treadmill to potentially relieve the stress that I was feeling. Some hours later, I calmed my nerves, collected myself, and laid back down. I did not know what could have caused this feeling within me; to make me feel so anxious and defeated. What was it? Why?

Then it dawned on me: the night previous to that morning, I had spent hours on my smartphone, on social media, random events, faces, lives, and different worlds. I drove myself towards insanity. I realized I had a problem. I realized why I was feeling so much anxiety and crankiness. I was spending so much time out of my life, on social media. That was it; it finally made sense to me. It made sense that these platforms were creating these types of mood swings, this negativity inside of me, keeping my mind always racing at the wee hours of the night and morning. As if social media became this virtual caffeinated dispensary. I think it is even stronger than coffee; it has a strong hook on you like an ocean current. I feel I should give these social media platforms other names; to make this story more interesting. Let's go with "Franklin Benjamin," "Ivory," "Twitchell," and "Sam Chapman."

I think you can understand which platforms I am talking about by the names. Hopefully, you can follow me and not be confused with the name replacement of these social media apps. Ivory was my drug of choice that night. Ivory was the one I used the most; where I had seen the most of other people. She had me hooked, more so than the others. We will get back to them later. But now, back to August 25th. I laid back down and managed to calm my nerves. Then I had a brief conversation with a friend of mine about what had happened. We talked; well, I should say we text.

As I quickly responded to my friend's text; that is when I entirely became aware; I had my Oprah, "*Uh, Huh*" moment. I realized that every time I received a notification, it released something inside of me. It released a feeling of urgency, a feeling of validation, and comfort. Comfort that someone who, even thou they cannot see my face, is thinking of me and reaching out to see what I am doing. The convenience of technology, right? As I was saying, that feeling: in a split second, you feel that you are of instant importance.

Now take that and apply that to social media. The likes, comments, tagged posts, and photos; the views, the followers, and even the un-followers. All of these notifications, not even counting the other notifications outside of your social media apps, emails, and what have you, are giving your phones a seizure every thirty seconds. How can we as human beings, continue to go through life like this; every single day for the rest of our lives? It is interesting how this virtual world is the new way of living, yet it is not living at all. What this new way of "existing" has become; is watching others live their "perfect" lives, which is their perfect lies. I could go on and on, and that is what I am going to do in detail. I hope as you are reading, you will put your phones on silent mode or at least on vibration.

I dedicate this journey to my parents, who brought me into this world: my family and the few friends I have. I would like to thank my former College English Professor; Henry "Hank" Stewart for teaching me the craft and art of creative writing; and to be fearless with what I have to write. I would like to also dedicate this book to Jaron Lanier, Cal Newport, and Tristian Harris. These men, considerable supporters in my decision to delete my accounts, and help me overcome my social media addiction.

1 *Like*

Just Give Me My Space

Myspace, that is where this whole nightmare started. I say nightmare because that is what social media was to me. But let me say this right now in the beginning. The majority of what I say and how I feel about social media is in no way to demonize these platforms or those who created them. I do not see social media as an evil thing, per se; it is just an app. However, an app on your smartphone, plus your free will, can turn into a horrific addiction, an addiction you would not even know you have. Some of you may have your usage of social media under control, more power to you. This story is solely my personal experience, and I chose to snap out of the self-hypnosis of scrolling up and down screens.

So, I got that out of the way; I now have my space. Well, I had a Myspace. In fact, I am sure a lot of people did back in the day. I guess I was around sixteen at the time when Myspace took over my life. It is incredible how I was even able to make an account and be active on it. I was a very shy and quiet young man. I did not talk much in high school; even though I was productive, I played football, wrestled, and had a few friends and associates. I still found myself in an anti-social state of mind, the internet was starting to emerge, and computers were becoming a man's best friend. Myspace was here! So, from what I remembered about my experience on Myspace, I opened up an account, uploaded a few profile pics, and sat around waiting for the notifications to emerge. Back then, I did not understand the "dopamine" release. But I will get back to that.

Myspace was exciting, I do have to admit. It was my introduction to this whole social media epidemic, and what did every Myspace account have in common? Tom! Tom Anderson was friends with everyone. A young Caucasian guy in the white T-shirt, smiling. To be young and wealthy through opening up a tech company, I would be smiling too. I find it mind-boggling how these tech gods created such seductive platforms. But I also realized that during this time, when I was on Myspace, I was just a kid. What the hell did I know what I was truly getting myself into back then?

Every day, when I logged into my account, I would see that icon light up, the spark of excitement, that thought in me saying, "oh wow, I got a notification." I was so naïve. If I could go back to this moment, this social media platform definitely would not have been the playground I had in mind. It was not even the case that I had many friends to begin with on this site. As I said, I only had a few friends and some casual acquaintances. So, to have a public account, showing other people parts of my life at an early age, how could I have known the consequences that would later come for me? But as I said, I was naïve. At that time, I was not sure what I wanted to do in life. I did not know what my future was to hold. No, I did; I knew I wanted to go to college. But I did not know what I wanted to study. I feel that maybe if I read more, educated myself on more options to choose from, my life would have taken a different journey. However, that was not the case because the hot trend of social media had seduced me. If I could go back in time to my sixteen-year-old self, I would have yelled, "STOP! Log off, delete your Myspace account right now, and never look back!" But I did not do that. I was not mature enough to know. So, I continued to stay active. I continued to post photos of myself, getting equipped with the new term "selfie."

"Selfies…" Good old-fashion selfies. Well, I guess selfies were around for quite a while; they were just not called selfies, probably self-portraits. But that was the thing to do: take selfies and upload them to your profiles. Set up your profile picture, so that other people know it is your profile, and help you stay connected. Make new "friends," if you will. I say "friends," in quotation marks, because it gave us the approval or the delusion of believing that everyone who sent us a "friend request" was indeed a friend. When I looked at my friends' list, some of those people I barely knew. Some I may have just had class with in high school, but never said a word to them. Keep in mind; I was that shy and quiet kid, so I did not have that many close friends in high school.

Oh, how could I forget about having family members as "friends" on Myspace? It is almost a downgrade to your family, in an awkward way. I look back on it; it was slightly weird to have family members that I would see often and have them looking at my profile. As if whatever I posted on

Myspace, was anything new to them. I would inform my family in person, what was going on in my life, rather than have them find out via Myspace. But that is not the case in today's social media world. You can say I became addicted to Myspace, opening my account every single day, patiently waiting to see the icons light up, and see those notifications. The My Mailbox; full of new messages, comments, new friend requests, invites, photo comments, blogs and birthdays; oh my God! To reminisce about all of this, I cannot believe I fell for these illusions of happiness, satisfaction, and validation. Where was I trying to go with all of this? Who was I trying to be? Better yet, who the hell did I think I was? It brought out specific behaviors that did not represent me. I was at that time, and still am to this day, a guy who minds his own business.

When I was on Myspace, I connected to all of these different profiles, some of who were random strangers (and you will hear the term, "random strangers," a lot throughout this book). I was spending-actually-wasting my time, I should say. I was wasting my time looking at other people's profiles, seeing who was friends with who, and who commented under this individual's picture, and other nonsense. What was I trying to gain or accomplish with all of this? I do not have a legit explanation. I was riding the waves like everyone else, not knowing that the boat I was on would hit rock bottom. Leaving me sinking and drowning in an ocean of confusion, and the deterioration of my character. I was not that guy behind the Myspace profile. I was an idea of who I thought I should be. A behavior I would not portray in my real life around people who knew me personally—taking pictures of myself that did not fit my character. I was trying to fit in with the trending look. Perhaps this was also the start of me not knowing myself, or even not liking myself. Not the best start for my life at the age of sixteen, going on seventeen and heading off to college. But My Space wasn't really going to be in my life for long, not because I was bored of it, but because I was about to be introduced to something much more powerful.

Another social networking website came from several brains of some college kids from Harvard University, a social networking website that was on the verge of changing the world, forever. That's right, Franklin Benjamin! Remember that I mentioned Franklin Benjamin earlier? That's what I'm calling this particular social networking website for the duration of this book. I also think you can understand why I gave it the name Franklin Benjamin, the fact of how much money this tech company has made in the last fifteen years. Not in any way to be derogative towards the company; this is to entertain you.

2 *Likes*

It's Nice to Meet You Franklin Benjamin (I hoped).

It was the year 2007, my freshman year in college. I attended Centenary University, which was Centenary College, back at that time. That was the year that I met Franklin Benjamin. Now being that I was addicted to Myspace, Franklin Benjamin was a smooth segue, especially having the same blue and white colors on their templates. I believe, in the beginning, it required that you had to be a college student or attended college to have an account. Now at first, I was amazed by Franklin Benjamin. It was a massive upgrade from Myspace. I cannot speak for you or anyone else, but for me, I practically abandoned my account on Myspace. Sorry, Tom! Franklin Benjamin felt much cleaner and innovative and also rewarding. On Franklin Benjamin, you get this reward; a digital prize every time you log on. An award that makes you feel good; that makes you feel great, right? Yes, the white and blue glove; the irresistible, instant validating "Like" button.

She's beautiful, isn't she? The more likes you get, the more aroused you become, the better you feel about yourself; at least that is how I felt at the very beginning. Those "likes" made me feel like I had an endless number of friends, more friends than I can even count. All it took was posting a photo and bam! Twenty likes in five minutes, twenty friends in the bag, right? Boy, I was so naïve about these social media platforms. To me, it felt like such an entity. But it did not just stop at the "likes;" I had the comments, the tagged photos, the birthday shout outs, and the "shared status post." I felt like a million bucks every single day.

I will be honest with you. It changed the dating game as well. I know you can relate to this. As a guy, freshman year in college, seeing all these different young women on campus, from all different walks of life. Franklin Benjamin was an excellent tool for me to use to open up and get comfortable to express myself to the public eye. Oh, do you remember the "poke" button? That creepy poke button. I was not a fan of that button, so I never used it unless someone poked me first and did not want to talk. But yes, some of my first encounters with women, I initiated on this social media phenomenon. I loved it more than a video game.

But why, though? Why did I "love" a social media website? Aren't we supposed to love people and living beings? Why did I love it? Did I love it because it helped me crack out of my shell and have some form of confidence, though this confidence only came from behind a laptop computer? Did I feel like it had matured me as an individual, thinking correctly, and making smart decisions? Who the hell was I, though? I had no idea. I was once again hooked on a new website, not thinking about the research papers I had to get done by the end of the week. I was not thinking about going outside, seeing the town of my new college, or even going around campus to get familiar with all the locations. I did not realize it then, but I regrettably know it now. I did not interact with anyone in college unless I used Franklin Benjamin. I talked here and there with people that I spent time with and who I was associated with on campus. However, at that time, there was a different kind of confidence between how I approached people in person and how I approached them online, especially women. I honestly did not like that. I did not like that at all.

So, the "likes" kept rolling in, as well as new friend requests and having the friend request I sent accepted from others. The unknown addiction was starting to grow in my mind, and I had no control over stopping it. It was like a compelling force. Not a force of nature, but this force of society; an effective plan, if you will. Oh, but let us not pretend that people on Franklin Benjamin never rejected us. I cannot tell you how many friend requests I sent out, and then being rejected. I will admit it; the rejections made me feel some type of way at that time. It made me feel like, "Wow, what the hell is their problem?" I had some ego back then, though it was a bit fragile. But don't we all? I guess I did not get social media. One would think that social media is a peaceful community, with positive, friendly people with open minds. But there is some deep ocean darkness within us, more than what I thought it to be.

Do not get me wrong; it did create some opportunities, sparked some friendships, and even companionships here and there. I cannot say that it was all just horrifying. But what I can say is that it was manipulating. I noticed a lot of funny things happening on Franklin Benjamin. By the way, I am sure by now, you no longer need to hear the name Franklin Benjamin ever time, so I will just use the initials "FB." FB was becoming more than a platform, not necessarily for exploiting your lavish lives and family photos, and so forth, but a platform of advertisements of multiple corporations. That was the most irritable occurrence I would see every time I logged in to FB, ads for new shoes, new services, or new furniture. For example, let's say you post a caption saying, "I have the biggest headache ever; feels like my brain is thumping." Almost immediately after posting that, you may come across an Ad for Tylenol, Aleve, or Bayer aspirin. You could also have a friend on FB comment with some sort of recommendation. But why do we need all of these ads on our profiles every single day? Back then, I did not know why, but I most certainly do now.

As I go back to the past and remember just seeing things online, everyone could not wait to post and gossip via FB. How about your favorite tv show, episodes that you have not watched yet, and one of your FB "friends" discloses the entire show or spills the beans on who died in the show? It practically defeats the purpose of you watching anything—same scenario when it comes to sports. FB changed the game. After college, FB did keep me in touch with a lot of people I met in the four years. I have met some fantastic people, but I have to be honest; when I still had a FB account, the connections I once had with "friends," were short-lived. It was a disconnect from the real relationships and bonds I had established with them.

When I look at it today, I find it so bizarre to have a friend you have not seen in years, yet you are "friends" on FB. You see each other's lives over the years, then all of a sudden you bump into each other out in the real world. Would you find it rather difficult to ask them how they are doing? Asking them, "how is life?" Especially when you have seen pictures of almost everything they have done in their lives. Marriage, weddings, children, or the unfortunate loss of loved ones. It is like you know so much about them now, without seeing each other for years. How do you get surprised or happy to see someone anymore? There is no real reason to ask friends questions when you see them; just log on to FB, "like" a few of their pictures and call that "staying in touch," right?

I can tell you that while I was on social media, it probably ruined more friendships or potential relationships then it created. Because I relied solely on social media to be that bridge, that kept me accessible to those people. I made FB responsible for maintaining a bond with friends, but unfortunately, and painfully, that was a mistake. You tend to see people's true colors very clearly on FB. You see the sarcastic comments people leave behind, people who are your "friends." You see adults talking and acting like kids, and kids cussing and indulging in adult activities. It is almost as if the roles have switched. I have never seen adults behave in such juvenile forms, making posts to one another about coworkers, and then the coworkers seeing rumors and spreading it around. Creating behaviors of what you would call today "cyberbullying." You would think that cyberbullying is something that cruel young kids would do. But oh no, grown adults in their forties, fifties and older participate in these childish acts. Slightly scary, I would say.

If this is what kids of the future will look up to, then we will be in a world that is not a world. But a living hell of cold-hearted people, with dark essences.

It is tough to even think of my life during FB. It was an active part of my life; I stayed loyal to checking it every single day. Checking my messages, seeing how many likes and comments I received—seeing that globe icon turning red and release the long-awaited dopamine. It felt great to have that every day, to feel that instant validation, and to get noticed by people you never thought you would. Maybe an old crush was liking your post or selfies, and you were feeling like, "oh my God, they are in love with me!" It reminded me of the feeling I had as a kid, waking up Christmas morning to open my presents. But as a college kid, I was waking up to open FB, to see the gifts of likes, comments, and new friend requests. It felt just like Christmas to me every single day.

Perhaps you may have had an experience; when there was someone on FB who was really in love with you. But you did not feel the same for them, you liked their post, and then that person had the wrong idea, sending out many mixed signals that accumulate with this platform. Now, not everyone will relate to my personal experiences with FB. However, I am undoubtedly positive that some will understand where I am coming from with what I am saying. Can you believe that in today's world, FB has well over two billion people and counting with active profiles? That is not even counting those who are no longer physically here with us.

That is another thing, those who have passed on. Our loved ones, our best friends, people we have worked with, or attended the same school. Those who passed away but had a FB account and their profile is still active; where you can see their photos, their post, everything up until their demise. It is like a virtual tombstone for them. Friends and family still posting comments under their profiles, saying, "We miss you." Then, over the years, all of the random ads, game invites, and spammed posts piling up and growing on their news feeds like a bunch of digital weeds. I always had a bittersweet feeling about profiles of the deceased still being accessible. It was nice to look at, to be reminded of them and the lives they lived, and how much love people had for them. Then there are the moments where you may be scrolling, and you see their profile come up, but it is one of those spam posts that is controlled by the bots and computer bugs. Think about how that can affect someone for the rest of the day or even you. It did affect me.

I was always active on FB; I would say the time I was overly productive on this site, is when I started pursuing a career as an actor. I started in the theatre at my college. The acting was and still is what cracked open my shell and helped me progress into the man that I am today. But after college, I switched to film and television acting, which meant I had to start over from scratch. I chose the hardest profession in the world. However, I did not see myself pursuing anything else. I love the work, being on set; the excitement and the different types of people I have met throughout the years; staying in contact with my acting friends through FB. It felt great to be able to post pictures of myself on set in wardrobe, portraying a role. Yet the problem with that was I fulfilled nothing by posting those moments. It was not like I was booking lead roles to A-list movies. I was doing a general background, photo double, and stand-in work. Posting a selfie of myself while I was on set was becoming a significant need to feel validated. To prove to my FB "friends," that I was making it when truthfully, I was faking it.

I was nowhere near where I wanted my career to be. Still, the power of perception on FB can make anyone look as if they are living the life of a millionaire. I was looking like the next Will Smith. Boy, those moments felt so monumental to me. But then I would get those questions in the back of my head; "What is the next thing I have to do? What is my next post going to be? How are you going to top that last selfie with Donnie Wahlberg or the one with Method Man?" I even felt as if I was putting this excessive pressure on myself that I had to keep up a particular routine. A specific image that made it look like more than what it indeed was. That is not to say I was not on set those times that I posted about; I was there. I just was not making it in the "big time." But I am a firm believer that a picture is worth a thousand words. I knew people were proud of me; I felt that for sure. But as the likes started to fade, the comments no longer came in, and everyone had moved on; I kept asking myself, "what is next?"

From my perspective, FB was a tool that I misused. I misused it by using it excessively. Too much of anything is good for absolutely nothing, and I had used this platform way too much. Maybe that is what I did not acknowledge about myself. But the fact that this platform does not shut down, a twenty-four hour, seven-days-a-week service to the public, and for free. How was I ever going to know the cognitive dangers that were waiting for me? There was no escape from this virtual perception of the good life, the constant aim, and pursuit of perfection. At that time, everyone was logged on to FB: Mothers, fathers, brothers and sisters, even grandparents in their seventies and eighties. Everyone was hungry for those likes and comments. I sure was, not even knowing that I was planting the seeds of my desperation, anxiety, and depression.

I remembered FB from before the smartphones, back when laptops were consuming our time in this innovative digital world. I remembered sitting in class at college, looking at those glowing blue lights from the laptop screens. It was as if UFOs were shining a light on the faces of my classmates, ready to pull them into their spacecraft and abduct them. If you think about it, that is pretty much an accurate analysis; metaphorically speaking. Those laptops were abducting our minds.

The internet, FB, and God know what else people were surfing the web for on those laptops. The internet has abducted our minds, our souls, and our desires for having a perfect life. That is what I now see it as—the combination of social media, emails, research papers, and online shopping. Laptops were the toys of the century until we were blessed and cursed with smartphones, the electronic organ that we cannot live without daily. Something that would make my skin crawl at times was when I would post on FB, a selfie, a status update, or just whatever I had on my mind for the day. Then afterward, I would get a phone call from my mother, who was a FB "friend," asking why I was feeling that way or why I posted that. I understood; mothers always care. But my God, could I just post something without being questioned, or have people worried about me? Family and your real friends are the only groups that you cannot bullshit or hide something from in your life.

Families always bust your bubbles on your profiles. You post all these new plans, ideas, dreams, and goals on FB. Then, your family and friends grow curious and interrogate you in real life. I am sure for some of you aspiring lawyers, someone in your family said this to you: "Wait, since when do you want to go to law school? I saw your FB post five minutes ago stating that you want to be a lawyer?" It is like you really cannot have your moment without negativity invading your account, which leads me to this epidemic of cyberbullying. Cyberbullying has reached an all-time high in our society; in fact, an entire planet of people who are on this platform.

Keep in mind; over two billion people log on every day. Random strangers, coming on your FB page, calling you every name in the book. Fat, ugly, a whore, a slut, pervert, "I hope you die, BITCH!" "That dress tho. LOL!" Do not even get me started with the bullying and shaming of people's sexuality. Let me tell you; before social media came into our lives and gave us a platform. I never thought human beings would be so unbelievably harsh and cruel to each other. I have never seen such disrespect in my life, and it has become worse. What possesses people to have absolutely no heart, no empathy, or compassion for people in the time of need? As if being kind to one another has grown to be an original sin? Is it no longer cool to be a human being anymore? What is the problem?

Now, this is not to say that some positive things are not on FB. There most definitely is kind, genuine, respectful enlightenment you can find on there. However, you can always find the rotten apple that spoils it for everyone. It is just amazing; those people out there, who are behind their laptops and smartphones. Typing their demonic fingers away on their keypads, letter by letter the cruelty of these "human beings," if that is who they are. I do not know based on the inhumane comments they leave on their "friend's" FB page. It makes you hate people sometimes. It shows the true colors of people, yet it also shows you who your real friends are, who loves you and cares for you.

I have had my share of receiving negative comments; thank God I only need one hand to count them on. Have you ever achieved or done something great, post about it on FB, then come across those individuals who would leave a comment under your post? You would think that person would say, "congratulations?" But what that person commented is a correction of a word you misspelled in your caption? Have you ever crossed paths with a "Friend" like that? Well, I have, and it just drained my energy when that happened. For example, I am an artist. Occasionally I draw and paint. One time I made a drawing of John Lennon and Yoko Ono. When I posted the picture to my FB page, I put in the caption, "John Lennon and Yoka Ono." People responded to it; likes, comments, and all those good things. Until that one individual commented, saying, "IT'S YOKO!" I saw that and said, "really?" I mean, okay, I get it, I accidentally misspelled her name. Still, that person saw the drawing, and something about it captured their attention. Nevertheless, instead of hitting that like button, that individual left a sarcastic comment. I guess not everyone is going to be excited about your achievements in the FB world.

There are many reasons why I deleted all of my social media accounts. One of the reasons is I realized that FB was changing me all across the board. It affected my mood throughout the day, every day. I was addicted to it, for reasons I did not even understand. Was it the "likes"? The comments of people saying, "congratulations," every time I had success? Did I just like seeing what everyone else was doing in their lives and me saying to myself, "I want that," "I want to go there," "Oh wow, she's beautiful!" But then I would be saying in my head, "What am I doing with my life?" "Why am I not where I want to be in my life, and everyone else is doing better than I am?" "Why do I not love myself anymore?" All these different thoughts were swirling swiftly through my mind like a merry-go-round. A merry-go-round of a bunch of crying babies, screaming and screaming at the top of their lungs. Anxiety and depression becoming my new worst friends. I did not ask for this to happen. I guess I became the one whose mind was abducted by that glowing laptop screen, shinning on my face back in college. FB had my attention, my mind, my heart, and even my soul. But it was far from over, once FB introduced me to Ivory, Twitchell, and Sam Chapman.

3 *Likes*

Ivory, Twitchell, and Sam Chapman

I am just going to start with Twitchell; Mr. Tweety Bird. I could not, for the life of me, understand the relevance of Twitchell. The white bird; well sometimes blue, depending on the background. The only reason I ever had a Twitchell account was for a class assignment in college. My professor insisted that the class opened up an account since we were living in the social media world now, and it was a must that we were active on this platform. I simply did not get it. People write a tweet, a caption with limited characters on how they are feeling that day. Afterward, people received heart-shaped "likes," "retweets," and maybe a few new "followers." That is it? That is all you can do? I mean, sure you can upload photos on there as well, but I am sure that FB and Ivory were the ultimate platforms to do so for that kind of attention. Keep in mind; I was never much of a talker. So as far as having something to say and tweeting about it and looking for some retweets and likes? I had no intentions whatsoever of using Twitchell, under any circumstances.

I am an actor; I have been pursuing a career for quite some time now. I can say that as of right now, I have been very fortunate to be in the position I am in, in this industry. I still have a great journey to travel, but I believe in myself enough that I will make my mark. I bring this up because I took an acting class some years ago. In this acting class, we had a casting director come in to take a look at the student actors' monologues. I volunteered to go first. I chose a speech from the movie "*American Beauty*," directed by Sam Mendes. There is a scene with the characters Ricky Fitts and Jane Burnham, played by Wes Bentley and Thora Birch. In the scene, Ricky and Jane are watching a home video that he recorded of a plastic bag floating in mid-air. As they watch, he is talking about life, how beautiful it is, if you just observe it from a different perspective rather than how society forces you to look. I am just giving you my take on it, and what I got out of that scene. It is one of the most beautifully done movies; my favorite film composer Thomas Newman did the Original Score for this film. I will talk more about Thomas Newman later. If you have not seen this film, it is well worth the time out of your life because sooner or later, you will understand that it will speak to your own experience, in some way.

The monologue I chose to do was that particular scene. I did not do so hot with performing this monologue; I must admit. It was not as effective as I could have made it, but hey, you live, and you learn. The casting director was not pleased with my performance and had no problems with expressing that. I received some constructive criticism and some rather harsh criticism. It comes with the territory. After I took my seat, I began to watch the other actors perform their monologues. Sitting behind the casting director, I could not help but notice that she was sitting there, on the phone, tweeting while the actors were doing their monologues. I was so disgusted, appalled even. We, as struggling artists, spend our hard-earned money on acting classes. Yet, this casting director does not have the courtesy to put her phone away and give her full undivided attention. Nothing urgent, just on the phone tweeting. I remember it like it was yesterday. The casting director looked up at the actor performing for five seconds, then looked back down at her phone, tweeting. Telling us students to go on Twitchell and tweet the hashtag, "*I don't play*!" The ego, the arrogance with this particular casting director. That was one of the worse experiences I have ever had in this business. I did not know tweeting was of that much importance for some people, that much of an addiction.

That was the last time I took an acting class. I never wanted to experience that ever again. It is amazingly sad how seriously people have taken these platforms, the sheer desire for attention and validation. People do or say whatever they have to just to make some noise, just like a baby in a crib crying out to get someone to pick them up. Actually, no, maybe not like a baby. A baby cries for their mother or father. People on social media cry for the attention of random strangers. The insanity of people having an opinion at the same time. People are tweeting about politics, religion, sexuality, and celebrities' personal lives. Everyone has an opinion on something that has absolutely nothing to do with them.

Everyone with a profile is an expert at something, whether it is some dating advice, parenting advice, or spousal advice. All these "gurus," "motivational speakers," and "influencers;" those types of brands seem like the thing to be today. Oh, we cannot forget the comedians; The "meme" era has turned the world into a comedic playground. Anything and anyone can be a "meme." Do not get me wrong; I found many of them quite funny at times. You do see the comedic genius in the people who create them. I have indulged in creating some memes, and the responses were great. But at times, comedy on social media can cause an inflamed backfire.

Prime example, some years ago, comedian/CEO Kevin Hart posted several tweets that I will not repeat. The tweets were considered homophobic. Kevin Hart was the guy to host the Oscars back in 2019. However, months before the Oscars, those same tweets resurfaced to grasp the attention of the general public. Out of nowhere, people were outraged—especially members of the LBGTQ+ community. Now, of course, for some people, what Hart said in those tweets were offensive. People demanded an apology from Kevin Hart. It went to the point where Kevin Hart respectfully had to withdraw himself from hosting the Oscars. I do not blame him for doing so; with his brand and a large following and other reasons, you do not want all that hard work deteriorating because of a few tweets. But I find it appalling how you can tweet something, from almost a decade ago, people will sit there for hours upon hours, scrolling through your page, and find those tweets that they can use against you. They exhumed Kevin Hart's tweets and made him pay for that. I feel that more people, especially celebrities, have lost many jobs and had to apologize many times because of what they had to say on Twitchell.

One of my supporters in deleting all of my social media accounts, a man by the name of Jaron Lanier, is an author, computer scientist, virtual reality pioneer, and has many other traits. It was over a year ago that I discovered who he is. Three weeks after I quit social media, I came across a video of Jaron on YouTube. He was on the ABC talk show, "The View," promoting his new book, "*Ten Arguments for Deleting Your Social Media Accounts Right Now*." Now I know that YouTube is considered social media. However, some of the videos I have come across have helped me be the human being that I am today. It gave me more insight and the ability to self-reflect. I, however, do not use it for social gains or branding. Because if I did, there would be no escape from my social media addiction. But at least those who do, receive some monetary compensation for their videos.

But Jaron is the guy who helped me, even though I have never met this man in person, at least not yet. Not sure if I ever will. But if he so happens to come across this book, I just want to say thank you to him for the support in helping me make my decision. Because of his support, I can move forward in life without the "*manipulation machine*," as he refers to social media. Jaron also calls these platforms "*behavior modification empire*s."

I brought up Jaron Lanier in this chapter because he mentions in "*The View*" that he sincerely believes Donald Trump is addicted to social media, Twitchell, in particular. Jaron Lanier also indicates that there is a third party behind the scenes that is manipulating you every time. These are not actual quotes; I am paraphrasing. But what I got out of Lanier's message was that you are under surveillance, always. Who would imagine? Perhaps that is what happened to Kevin Hart. He could have been watched consistently by a third party, to sabotage his opportunity to host the Oscars, and to manipulate the public and set up a plot to assassinate his character. Who knows, right? This whole third-party scenario reminds me of "The Wizard of Oz." Someone behind a curtain, controlling and manipulating the masses in secret and who also claims to be the most righteous.

The thing is I cannot assume that everyone who uses social media has an addiction to these platforms. I feel that I can only speak for myself in this situation, and I was addicted to social media. I can say that now, which brings me to Ivory. The social media app with the camera icon as the symbol, the one Franklin Benjamin fell in love with and decided to buy.

Now I must say that Ivory was my favorite, but when I say favorite, I mean the most addicted. Not a day, not an hour went by that I did not check my Ivory account. It became much more frequent when smartphones came into place. But Ivory; that was my digital drug of choice. I would say every five minutes I was checking my account, looking to see my new likes, new comments, and new dopamine releases. I could not get enough of Ivory. Following any and every public profile of my preference. Following my favorite celebrities, my favorite health gurus, motivators, inspirations, models, food pages, religious, and political pages. Anything I desired or that was of interest to me, I followed them.

It came to a point where the ratio of how many people I followed, was triple the amount of who followed me. That meant I had a very long news feed that I looked through every single day, scrolling, and scrolling, and scrolling, with devotion. Sometimes it felt as if I went deaf or even paralyzed. I thought that I was hypnotizing myself by scrolling up my news feed so much. I was, without a doubt, hooked. Oh, did I love seeing that heart notification; appearing and disappearing while I was scrolling. I would quickly check it to see who showed me "love," attention and validation. I was obsessed with it, fascinated even. I was becoming another person, like some personality dysfunction.

I did not know who, as a person, I was or who I was becoming. There were plenty of times I would take different selfies from different angles, and then I would post one. I would let several hours go by and post the same selfie but from a different perspective. All those likes kept coming and coming, yet I was not satisfied. I wanted more, and I posted more. I guess I wanted more attention. Thank God I did not go to the extreme of what the youth would call "trolling" or "clout chasing," where I am an agent of chaos, causing trouble to seek more attention and more followers. I most certainly had a problem. But another problem on top of that; I had no one, at that time, to show me or tell me I had a social media addiction. I took no breaks from these platforms. I would place anywhere between 15-30 hashtags under my post, just to draw in random profiles to add on the number of likes I would receive regularly.

I was in full form now. I remember when I would go on the set of television shows and films; I would see some celebrities, movie stars that I used to watch as a kid. I would always, when the time was right, introduce myself and ask for a picture with them. Most of them would always say yes. When I look back at that now, I honestly regret that I did all of that. Celebrities, movie stars, athletes, whoever they are, keep in mind that they are still human beings just like anyone else. They are not animals at a zoo.

They breathe the same air as us, live different lives, yes, but they are still people with feelings and who need their time and space. If I could go back, I do not think I would have asked anyone for a photo. I would have just said, "Hello, how are you? Nice to meet you." Then I would just keep moving. What was I thinking? Back to what I was saying about random strangers, I was that random stranger to those people, asking them for a picture, and we do not even know each other. For what? For more likes and followers? Here I am using these people's fame, like a coupon, to gain some digital treats that are about as valuable as Monopoly cash. It was not professional at all.

The most ironic thing that happened to me on Ivory; the more likes and followers I started to gain, the more unhappy I began to feel. Now how can that be? I was supposed to be motivated to have more, excited. But the more and more I had, the less satisfied I became. I could not fuel my engine of satisfaction by any means. I was painting a picture of great success, bliss, and happiness. But deep down where the camera could not snap a shot, I was miserable and depressed. I was not a happy young man. I did not even know what happiness was. I would post a photo edited selfie to my page, gain likes, have women comment saying, "so handsome," "congrats," emojis, and be happy. But the validation was short-lived. I felt as if there was no escape from this. I thought that I had to keep this going for my acting career, to stay in touch with my friends. Yet my 'friends" were beginning to hit that unfollow button on me. When I found out, I took it the wrong way. I took it personally and felt that the bond that I thought was so strong with those individuals were not strong at all, but very fragile and swiftly evaporating.

Maybe there never was any bond. Just a tolerance of my social media presence. Plenty of times, people I have met would say, "what is your IG?" We exchanged profiles and "connected." About a week or so later, those same people unfollowed me. Why? Why would people ask for your IG account and then unfollow you right after? What were they looking for but did not find? I have no idea. One of my favorite poets, James Douglas Morrison, said it best, "*People are strange*." We cannot help ourselves, I guess. We have our mood swings, our good days, and bad days. Some days we want attention and love; other days, we want to be completely isolated. People vent on social media; I had partaken in that, at certain moments. Just a quick way to seek attention. But I never got into debates via social media, that I was not going to waste my time doing.

That is another issue too. You could be friends with someone for years. You have a debate with them online, and the next thing you know, that "friend" blocked you on all social media platforms. Just because you disagreed on social media, the friendship comes to an end. I have also experienced that before. It has a way of unleashing this hidden anger inside of you where you cannot wait to respond and retaliate, commenting the most heinous, volatile, unfavorable exchange of words. Just to be spiteful to one another. It is like virtual road rage. I believe we have lost a lot of the act of kindness. We are so involved with spreading rumors about each other. Neighbors are growing cruel intentions towards themselves. One is a Republican, and the other is a Democrat. One is a conservative, and the other is a liberal. We cannot even get along that much anymore. Of course, some of us are still genuine, kindhearted human beings. But when it comes to those behavior modification empires, as Jaron Lanier calls them, the dark side is there waiting for you at every scroll.

Another thing about Ivory that kept me hooked and addicted was the virtual seduction of the sexual exploitation of women. There are too many women on Ivory, who are just delivering these sexual, arousing pictures that draw not only the men in but also the women as well. The men, well, for obvious reasons. But the women, I feel that some women like to compliment themselves on how they look. Yet unfortunately, other women are comparing their looks, their bodies, to the next woman. Now I do not believe every woman will compare herself to other women and get discouraged about how they look. The proof is in the pudding, and you see the changes that women make to themselves, and respectfully so. Women have every right to do as they please, with their bodies.

However, it seems that many women believe that surgical procedures are the ultimate answer to achieving beauty. To be perfect; to look in the mirror and see flawless perfection. Posting away, to receive thousands of likes, millions of followers. Some women simply do not accept their body, they have a problem with how they look, and they want to change that. A woman has that right to do what she wants, especially if she is using her own money, her body her choice. Women are making changes to their bodies and then connecting that with social media; for the attention, more likes and comments than they could ever dream of achieving. Women would then become addicted, not just to the validation on social media, but to the modification of her anatomy. Social media and plastic surgery are beginning to go hand and hand, in the same bed. These young ladies are getting younger and younger, when it comes to going under the knife, and that is extremely frightening.

If or when I have a daughter, I fear that she will be exposed to things far more atrocious then what is happening online as of today. I fear she would feel that she is not enough. Not enough for society, not enough for herself. I fear she would think; the only way she could feel love is by receiving likes from random strangers who will never even know her. People who will never know her for who she is in her heart. I fear if social media is still around when she is old enough to understand how to use it, she will get seduced into the lifestyle of social media. She will feel compelled to expose herself to the general public, that instant gratification, many validations, everlasting comments, and the anxiety-producing "sliding in her DM's." I hope and I pray that she will make better choices than I did, for her own life. Because I, as her father, will be there to guide her in the right direction. I will be her compass.

Another thought I had about what women go through on those platforms is their bodies, and their looks are desperately worshipped. Still, their perspectives on life, society, politics, or even sports, are completely ignored. Women are only respected by their beauty when it comes to social media. A woman could post a bikini picture, showing her curvy, voluptuous body, and it goes viral. Let that same woman have a voice. Let her voice her opinion about the world, and there will be complete silence on her page unless there are other women showing support. A woman's body is what gets attention on social media, but her mind is entirely unappreciated and overlooked; over and over again. Some women may not find that to be true. Maybe that is not the case for some women personally. However, to you, women, I challenge you to study your post on Ivory one day. If you realized that you are receiving more likes on the pictures of your beauty than the likes you receive on, let's say, a quote, perhaps? You will then know what I am saying is accurate. I feel that to be so sad in today's world. I will try my best to start calling women smart, brilliant, a genius even, more often than I will call women beautiful. Not that women cannot be both, but I will try to pay more attention to a woman's intellectual abilities from now on.

I have looked into a lot of women's eyes before. I see a lot of things in their eyes too. A person can never hide what is in their eyes unless they are wearing shades, of course. That is why I never wear shades. I always want to look into people's eyes, and they look into mine. That is how I believe you can tell who they indeed are. Though I do wonder, what does a woman see through her eyes when she scrolls up and down her social media feed? Is she being respected by those random strangers? Is she loved and adored by many, or is she being crucified by the harsh demonic souls who comment in the most despicable languages you could think? Calling her fat, ugly, or her breast and butt are fake; everything about her is false. They may seem like simple derogatory terms, yet they are still the most painful. I am sure that it is excruciating when women see it in the comments section of their social media profiles.

These platforms have changed the way women entertain the world, your favorite celebrities, models, and actresses, or even just your everyday girl next door. When I was active on Ivory, I was definitely in tune to their entertainment, until I began to see women differently, the way they were looking very unreal in their photos. The aim for perfection was and still is getting out of hand. If a man were to fall for a woman that he sees via social media, he is not falling in love with her, but with an image of that woman, an idea of who he thinks she is, or who she thinks she is. Today it seems like it would not even matter who you are, on the inside. It would be just an; "he sees it, he likes it, he wants it, NOW!" Slides into her direct message and let the chips fall where they may. Next thing you know that woman behind the profile is not the real person, but a "catfish." I am sure that many of you had a catfish experience online.

Mark my words; you probably already know this yourself. Fifty years from now, your grandkids are going to ask you how you met your significate other. Some of you will say, "I slid in your grandmother's DMs." You know that to be true. It is complicated to maintain a long-lasting relationship while having these social media sites. The temptation is thick in the air, in the eyes glaring down in those screens, the ability to hide any evidence of proof that you were unfaithful.

That leads me to the last social media avenue, where I stopped before I went on a permanent vacation from this nightmare. That is Mr. Sam Chapman, another waste of time. So now I had Franklin Benjamin, Twitchell, Ivory, and Sam Chapman, all activated twenty-four hours a day, seven days a week. Four social media platforms in my life, dictating and manipulating me every step of the way. It was like I was a puppet controlled by these four strings; the north, south, east, and west were fulfilled, like witchcraft. Sam Chapman had second to no valve to me. If these four platforms were in a race for my time and attention, Sam Chapman was in third place. Wow, it is funny that I say these social media platforms competed for my time and attention. Because in a way, they, without a doubt, really were. Each one had its method of madness to fuel my addiction. Of course, others were much stronger, but I still made time to check all four.

If midnight was the beginning of my breaking point, I was at 11:56 p.m. I was falling down a spiral that I could not climb my way out. I could not even ask for help. Who was I going to talk to; that had a solution to my addiction, which led to my depression? Not my family or friends; they used social media just as much as I did. Who could I run to for help? Then the worst happened. I begin to post things that subliminally were a cry for help—crying for unnecessary attention—one too many selfies in a single day. On Sam Chapman, I would just record a video of myself doing nothing. Nothing, just to see who would open up my stories and get the number of views. That was another problem I created for myself. I was paying attention to the numbers, which I will elaborate much more on. I would usually see the same group of people see my stories on Sam Chapman, which I will simply say "SC" now.

The same people; it was not as if I had much communication with SC. It had no meaning or value to my life, but the addiction was already there. It was already at a point of no return. I would just be on it, looking at what everyone else is doing with their lives—living their lives, going out to parties, and on dates. It sounds like I did not have a life, right? Maybe that is because I did not at that time. My life only consisted of pretending to be someone else or too much dreaming and not enough doing and not feeling that I was enough. The merry-go-round of crying babies was still in my mind, stronger and louder than ever before. I now had four avenues of self-destruction. It was getting worse; my addiction, I mean. I was getting to the point of no return. I would start living in a vicarious state of mind—living through others' life experiences—seeing people travel the world and desperately imagining that I was there. I imagined lying on a beach in Jamaica, flying to London, riding on a double-decker bus through the London bridge, taking a picture of Big Ben. Then I head over to Tokyo, taking a selfie next to the Tokyo Tower.

That is what I would envision based off of the photos I see other people take. Random strangers that took snap shots of where they have been to; that I have never traveled to before. That was all I needed; more fuel to keep the depression alive and growing. My God; the paranoia in me, the confusion of who I was at that time. It was a feeling of my life not belonging to me. My life now belonged to these four platforms. Social media was so close to robbing me of my love for acting and the film industry that I had been working in for several years at the time. As I said before, I was more focused on just taking selfies and pictures with celebrities so I could upload them to my accounts. I did not even care as much; I was not as happy as I seemed to be in my photos. I would not say that I was going insane, but I imagined that I was going somewhere, thinking I was about to make it big just by getting likes on a photo. Trying to impress people, I was most definitely flirting with insanity.

It was becoming official; I did not love myself. I was exploiting an idea of who I thought I was or should be through those selfies, the quotes, the memes, and the screenshots of me featured on the television shows. I exploited this man that was not me because I thought he was so cool. I thought he was a star. He was the guy that I was really living vicariously through, day by day; that guy that people saw on social media was not the guy they met in real life. I admit that now. That guy on those platforms thought he had all the answers. I gave that guy my face for photos, my name, my ideas, my goals, and my dreams. What did that guy give me in return? Short-lived friendships, paranoia, lustful desires, anxiety, depression, likes, comments, views, and followers, but no happiness. No satisfaction or validation at all. To be honest, I did not feel a damn bit of good while I was in this nightmare. I honestly did not.

I did not feel anything for anyone anymore, not even myself. I stopped wishing people a happy birthday. I stopped interacting with people who said beautiful things to me and took them for granted at times—numbed to actual human feelings. I could look at videos of people fighting, people hit by cars, or even shot and killed. I would feel nothing. How could that be? The guy that I knew myself to be would feel much compassion and empathy for people.

But in that social media world, people were nothing more to me but just numbers. That guy was not me; that was not Jordan Wells: the man, the human being. My soul was utterly missing in this virtual world, and I did not have the slightest idea of how to find it and be reunited. That is until I realized that I knew where my soul was. My soul was right inside of my pocket. My soul; trapped inside my phone, where I unintentionally placed it. My whole identity was on my phone. Oh my God, now I know why I always heard my phone ringing, even when it was on vibrate, and why I was continuously checking for it when I did not have my phone with me. That was my soul saying, "GET ME OUT OF HERE!!!."

4 *Likes*

Stupid Me; Smartphone

I now pronounce you: social media and smartphone; you may now kiss the addiction. Once social media became these little entities called "apps," downloaded to a smartphone, that was it. For me, at least. I knew my addiction to social media would never die after this brilliant, unstoppable accessibility was in order. These pocket-sized electronics, with four social media applications, in the palm of my hand. Lord have mercy on me and the rest of the world. Every five minutes, hell, every two minutes, I was checking my phone for notifications. The sound notifications, I even selected different sounds for different apps; so that I knew which social media platform was sending me some of those attention glitches. It was a whole new experience from having social media on a laptop. With a smartphone, you can check your status everywhere you go. Everywhere; your car, your bathroom, hell, even your wedding or funeral.

I believe when Apple founder, the late Steve Jobs, introduced the world to the very first iPhone, he was aware of the dangers that waited for us consumers. I wonder had he still been alive today, what would his feelings be towards social media and how it became a huge necessity to all smartphones? It is a scary society that we live in today.

Take about twenty seconds; right now, from reading this, look up and around you at this very moment. Has it been twenty seconds? Okay, good, so what did you see? I bet you saw a bunch of people looking down at their smartphones, seeing that glowing blue light on their faces. Seeing their thumbs scrolling and taping away on those screens. Or maybe, you just saw a friend you have not seen in a long time, or perhaps you just missed your train stop. You may even see me. No, I am just kidding. You could see many things. But if I had to bet my last dollar on it, I am confident you will see a lot of people, heavily engaged on their smartphones. I believe I will be accurate with that.

These smartphones have us, and the relationship it has with social media, these smartphones own us. It is where we keep our passwords, our credit card numbers, our photos, Face IDs, even our thumb and fingerprints now. Smartphones and social media have changed the world, and they have changed us, people. We are literally in bed with our smartphones. They are the electronic teddy bears. We check them at night before we go to bed, if we ever go to bed, right? Then we go right back to them again when we wake up. Be honest, what is the first thing you do in the morning?

I bet you turn around to your nightstand and check your smartphone, to see who liked your last tweet, your previous post, or a text, or email. I had that problem for sure. I could not even get up to use the bathroom before I checked my phone. My smartphone became an organ outside of my body, that I could not leave behind or not be too far away from, distance-wise. It was sickening to live like that. That urge to take my smartphone with me every step of the way. What the hell was wrong with me? I could not even go two feet away, from one room to the other without my smartphone. I remember times when I could hear my phone ringing, I would listen to the notifications, and I would run up my stairs just to see who was calling. Only to find out my phone was not ringing at all. Once again, my soul was screaming to me, "get me out of here!" But I did not know how to breakthrough. You hear those notifications so much every day; you can hear the sounds even when your smartphone is off.

Why do we call them "smartphones" anyway? It is bad enough that we, as human beings do not call ourselves smart that often, but we have no problem calling these human-made products smart. Perhaps someday, another genius will invent "smart guns." I will let you sit on that one and think about it. I have had several of these "smartphones" in my life, from Androids to iPhones. What I have learned about these products is; they are tools. Tools that we should use and not have them use us. I remember when I had the latest phone that came out, then people would ask me how I feel about my new phone, and I would say, "I love my new phone." Love? How do I love something materialistic; that can be replaced, but only like people? I should love people and only like things.

I had my priorities twisted. Do not get me wrong about these phones; I am pleased that they exist. The way technology has changed our world. We can hold on to those cherished moments of our families, record newborn babies, documenting your child's first steps, weddings, or even proof of heinous acts of racism and police brutality on video. We have it all; we have the whole world in the palm of our hands. Every one of us now has power in the palm of our hands and boy do we want to use that power. But the downfall is that many people in this world use that power for corruption, greed, and solely for attention.

I believe that smartphones are going to be able to do just about anything except being a phone. I believe one day in the future, these products will be these little machines that think for us, plans our future for us, and even aligns us to our destiny. I believe the innovators of the future will create a new smartphone; that could take fourth-dimensional snapshots of infants at the age of one. The highly advanced software of this new smartphone will have the technological ability to develop a concept or idea of how those infants will look by the age of fifteen.

Let's say that this new "smartphone" would predict how a baby girl will look by the age of fifteen. The device will create a concept image that predicts the baby girl will be a gorgeous young lady. The device will then be able to connect the parents of that baby girl to agencies for modeling or acting. The agencies would be able to see the concept image and make a decision on whether or not to get in contact with the parents of the child. Keep in mind; it is just a one-year-old baby girl; who has not yet even realized she exists. This smartphone would connect the parents of that baby girl to agencies, merely banking on the potential of what she perhaps, may look like in the future. Catch them while they are young, right?

These new devices would be able to do that for an infant's intelligence as well. They could give your infant child an IQ test that would determine the intellectual future of your child. The innovators could design features in these new smartphones that predicts what we want to eat and already have it delivered to our homes. These devices would be able to send our friends messages saying, "I miss you, let's talk soon," even though we were not thinking about that particular friend. Still, the device will know we have not spoken to that friend in a long time, so it reaches out for us.

What is even scarier than that is these new devices could predict our deaths. These new smartphones could tell just how much longer we will have left to live, right down to the second to last, of our heartbeats. Once we take that last breath, the morticians would already be on their way, ready to pick up our bodies. Our information, our death certificate, would already be on file, logged in, done deal. If you were to have social media as well on these devices, it would show up on your friends' news feed as "breaking news," and show your face along with your birth date and death date. It would be as if these new devices would be our whole lives. They would suck the souls right out of our bodies. No kids at school; their devices would teach them one by one. No doctor appointments needed; just place your new smartphone in your mouth and let it scan your entire oral area. It would check for sore throats, thyroid problems, or even your temperature.

Yes, that sounds like a smartphone to me. Everything you could want or need would be right there, in the palm of your hand, at the push of a button. That is what I believe could potentially happen in the future. The disconnect to stay connected. To be honest, we are not that far away in today's world from what I envision in the future. Even though I do not like to predict things, these smartphones can keep an infant locked in and hooked. The new babysitter is what I call these phones. Every time I see an infant with one of these devices in their hands, the babies are getting controlled instantly.

How does an electronic device have more control in keeping a child still, than the actual parent? I went into a grocery store one day, I grabbed a few things, and went on the line to check out. Two shopping carts in front of me, there was a mother with her infant child. The baby had to of been a year old at least. The baby was watching something on their parent's smartphone. If you could have, just saw the look on that baby's face, how that baby engaged with that phone. The baby had a grip on that phone, tighter than any anaconda ever had on its prey. It was like the baby was getting possessed by that phone. Now that I think about it, I cannot recall the last time I saw a baby with a bottle in their hand or a toy at least. All I see are these electronic gadgets in their little hands. If these devices can keep an infant child calm, preventing the baby from crying, what do you think it is doing to the kids and adults of society?

Ever since I logged off of social media, I am barely on my smartphone. I do not use my phone often; that way, my head is up, and I am looking at my surroundings. Now, I am on the other side of the fence. Let me tell you; when I see other people surrounding me, I feel as if I am in the twilight zone.

I see people with their heads down, looking into the glowing blue-lit screens, the same glow that I would see on my college classmates' faces from their laptops. I see a Déjà vu all over again, and it is everywhere. I see adults, senior citizens in their seventies and eighties, I see teenagers and babies. All in that one position of their heads down, one arm bent holding their phones. After deleting all of my social media, I knew my smartphone use would plummet. I also knew that I was going to be like an outcast. Someone on the outside looking in. In the beginning, I felt like a lonely man. I felt like I was this ghost in the digital world who was not getting with the program. I felt like no one could even see me. I felt like if I were on fire, no one would try to save me, but they most definitely would record me as I burn. That brings me to a topic, a real tragic event that I thought about some time ago, and how these smartphones have done something to the souls and minds of us human beings.

If I may, let us go back in time to the tragic, horrifying events of September 11th, 2001. Let me just say before I go forward; in absolutely no way, am I trying to make light of this painfully sad, devastating day. Please forgive me if it comes off in such way. I wish this horrifying event never, ever happened. This world has never been the same ever since. I have not been the same ever since. My heart goes out to every victim who lost their life, and to all the families who lost a loved one. You may be asking yourself; "what does September 11th, 2001, have to do with social media and smartphones?" Well, let me create a vision for you, for you to understand. Let's say that the events of the September 11th terrorist attacks, did not take place in the year of 2001, but in the year 2019. The social media era. The way people just whip out their phones today and record videos of just about anything you could think of and then some. People do not stop to think about what they are recording; they only record for the likes and views. If someone gets hit by a car or train, they record. If someone gets shot, they record. If someone were to fly a plane into a building, in the year 2019, what do you think those same people would have done?

That is correct; they would have recorded. If the September 11th attacks happened in 2019, instead of people running for their lives, people by the thousands would have flocked towards the towers. People would have pulled out their "smartphones," aimed up at the flames, and press that record button. Social media would have gone into a frenzy. It would have crashed in a matter of minutes, or would it? It stays open all day every day. People would have recorded dozens of video footage, hundreds, thousands of photos, upload them to their iCloud, social media profiles, YouTube channels, and collecting ads. My God; just imagining if that day happened in today's time with theses smartphones. I believe some people would just have not cared. They would have recorded every second. Yes, I am sure in their minds, some people would have thought how horrible this is. But in the back of the mind of others, they would have thought, "I am going to get over 20 million views easily."

Some people would not even stop to think about how soulless filming all of this would have been. People all over the city would have stopped where they stood, and record; people all over Manhattan, Queens, Staten Island, Brooklyn, and New Jersey. Everyone would have looked like statues, holding up those smartphones. To be honest with you, I believe that if 9/11 occurred in 2019, more people would have lost their lives, because instead of people running for their safety, they would have been more concerned about recording everything. The evil trolls of social media would have created their demonic memes, highly offensive captions under their post. It would have been mortifying, scrolling up and down the social media news feeds, seeing those images of that day, over and over. People would report as they go live on their platforms, pointing fingers, blaming whoever. The American people would hold Donald Trump responsible. Could you even imagine what Trump would say about all of this, had this tragedy happened while he is in office? Yea, neither could I.

However, if 9/11 had unfortunately occurred in 2019, with these smartphones, those who lost their lives would have been able to make a final video recording of themselves. Those who were on United 93, those trapped in the towers could have made contact with their loved ones for one last time. Facetimed their families, leave voice messages for their families and friends to hear them and hold on to their voices forever. Firefighters, victims under the rubble would have been rescued sooner. Damn, I wish this never happened to those innocent people on that day of inhumanity. That day we got a massive bite of harsh reality.

The moral of this chapter is we as people; we have to be the smart ones, instead of relying on "smartphones" to be our everyday compass. Find the balance between digital time and quality time. Allowing an electronic device to dictate your lifestyle is inhumane. I had to find my balance with my phone after I deleted all of my social media apps. But to be honest with you, after I deleted those apps, my use for my cellphone became eighty percent useless. Now, the twenty percent of the time I use my phone is to make a phone call, answer a text message, or look at an email. I will listen to music on occasion.

Since I do not have social media anymore, I rarely use the camera on my phone. I do not recall how much time I spent on my phones while I was using social media, but I am sure it was hours out of each day. Without social media, my phone usage, on average, is now between fifteen to thirty minutes per day. It is incredible; when I look at it now. Smartphones are practically time sponges. Just ready to soak in every last drop of your time. These devices want time from your sleep, time from your dates, your kids, your studies, and time away from your life period. By the way; look up again for another twenty seconds. Do you still see people on their smartphones? You see?!!! It is unbelievable what our society has become after social media and smartphones. With my addiction, there is no telling what I would have done if I still indulged in those addictive apps.

As far as being addicted to smartphones, I am really speaking from my own personal experience. I was addicted to my smartphone while I had active social media accounts. I do not believe that every person who owns a smartphone is addicted to them. However, you can now see the time spent on your devices for yourselves. I hated the fact that I was addicted to these products. These electronics, how could I be addicted to an electronic device? But then again, there is video game addiction, pornographic addiction, and even addiction to television. You have to keep products addictive in order for consumers to come back for more. It is not like an electronic; a television, a tablet, or a smartphone, where you can just buy one and be set for the next 4-5 years. Products such as cigarettes, pills, foods, and drinks; you have to keep those products addictive, with addictive ingredients. Otherwise, people would just buy the products once, and that would be it. Companies would not survive, they would plummet. Those are the specific reasons why we cannot stop eating those foods, drinking the alcohol, and still smoke. To relate that analogy to social media, they give people rewards;

the blue verified checks, the likes, the donations, the views, the notifications. Brilliant! Absolutely brilliant! Masterminds at its best.

Our brains are unique in how they operate. We have many random thoughts that run through our minds every single day. Numerous emotions that we cannot control. So, take our thoughts, our feelings, place a smartphone in our hands with social media; what you now have is a potential emotional hurricane waiting to happen. For example, let's say you open up a social media app; let us go with "Ivory." You open Ivory up, and the first thing you see is a post of your friend who just got engaged. You double-tap on your screen and comment, "Congratulations!" You are "happy" for them. Five seconds later, you scroll up to see another friend of yours, who posted about their mother, who recently passed away. Now you are "sad" for that friend, and comment, "I am so sorry for your loss." Another five seconds after that, you see a meme that is hysterical, and now you are "laughing." Do you understand what just happened there? You went through three different emotions; happy, sad, and laughing in a matter of fifteen seconds.

Imagine being on your social media applications for an hour. That is three thousand, six hundred seconds. Do you know what that can do to our brains? Do you ever wonder why people are so angry, so cranky, paranoid, or even so depressed? Why is negativity at an all-time high? Some people are on social media two or three hours a day; what can you say to that? There is no hard break from these products. There were times I was on social media for hours. All of the scrolling; all of that irrelevant information that seduced me to get my time. It left me empty on the inside. I had nothing to offer. Not to my followers or even to myself. Yet I still kept scrolling, thinking of the next big post, the post that just might help me go "viral." My next post to exceed my numbers of likes, views, and followers. These are the numbers to focus on, right? Wrong; I was consequently wrong.

5 *Likes*

What's Your Number?

Why were these numbers all of a sudden so important to me? To any of us, for that matter? The number of likes on each post, the number of views and subscribers you have on YouTube, or the number of followers you accumulate. Why is that so important today? Are the more followers you have on social media, the more validated you feel about yourself? If someone were to speak their minds on Twitchell about politics, receives over a thousand likes and retweets, does that person now think their opinion is validated? Why do we place people on a pedestal, based on a number presented through an app? I honestly believe that eighty percent of people's followers are bots and avatars; or even ghost followers.

Take your favorite celebrity's profile; for example, let's say your favorite star that you follow has ten million followers. Please take a look at the ratio of the number of followers they have, to the average number of likes they receive on their post. You would see that on every post, only twenty-five percent of their followers are giving likes. I bet you have never seen a person's profile, where half of their followers are active and liking their post, not even thirty-five percent. It is not all real; do not get me wrong; there are some good things; some of the interactions are real and trustworthy. However, I feel that we take these numbers that social media provides for us more seriously than we really should. As I said earlier, the more likes and followers I received, the unhappier I felt.

I have a theory about the number of likes. I am sure many may disagree, and that is fine. But let us put this scenario together. Let's say there's a mother who just gave birth to her newborn baby. This mother may only have a thousand followers at the most. The mother takes a few snapshots and posts a picture of her newborn on Ivory. Let's say the mother only receives 23 likes in the first five hours of posting her newborn baby. She has a thousand followers, but only 23 likes on her newborn baby's post. Then the next day, the number of likes only increased by ten, so now the picture has 33 likes. Wouldn't you think that mother would feel a sign of disgust and embarrassment? She shared with the world her newborn baby, the most important day of her life, and she only received 33 likes in 24 hours? With maybe several people commenting, "congrats!" I believe that the mother would feel a certain kind of way. The mother may think in her mind, "damn, is there something wrong with my account? Do people not think my baby is beautiful? All I get is 33 likes?"

Then afterward, the mother may post another picture of her newborn, this time from different angles. Maybe even post a video, so that way, she can see a higher number; through the views instead of the likes. If you post pictures of your meals when you go out, but do not receive many likes on that post, does that food still taste delicious to you? Hell; by the time you get finished posting your meal, trying to figure out the right caption, your dinner is probably already cold. Those numbers have a way of manipulating us on how we are supposed to feel about ourselves and our lives. Our success, our families, and our friends. Be honest; how many times have you posted and deleted something because it did not fill your quota of "likes?" When your post did not receive as many likes as you would of, liked.

Honestly, the only "numbers" I am focused on in my life today; are the numbers in my bank account and the numbers of my credit score. The ones I see in my blood work; to keep me healthy and alive. The number of years that I live on this earth. Also, how about the number of years people have been married? Those are the real numbers that we, as human beings, need to focus on most importantly. I find it so disturbing, when adults in their forties and fifties talk about how many likes their last selfie had, or how many views their video received. "It went viral!" The priorities in the adult world have become mortifyingly elementary.

Let me set up a scenario for you. You see a person's profile, and you look at their numbers. You observe the number of their followers and the number of people they follow. Be honest; have you ever seen those numbers and noticed that the person is following three times the number of people that are following them and think to yourself, "oh, this person isn't shit!" "This person is a weirdo; I'm not following them back." I am sure you have come across those types of profiles before. You cannot deny those numbers at the top of your accounts, do not dictate how people treat each other online. I genuinely believe that there are some "interesting" people out there who would rather have a million followers, over a million dollars. Those numbers from social media have contaminated our minds. People have defined those numbers to be of value to their lives. The numbers have defined our purpose in life and our importance to random strangers. The significant digits, the blue verified checks; just another way to boost a person's ego and call that success. I would hate to imagine what would happen if the numbers went on a decline. You may not take the numbers that seriously, which is a good thing for sure.

The way I saw numbers on my social media account, I did not care much for the idea of going viral. As I said multiple times, the more likes and followers I received, the unhappier I became. There was no satisfaction in those numbers for me. Because of my addiction, I always wanted to see notifications light up the screen on my phone. Every time I opened my phone and saw those hearts; who liked this post on FB and who viewed my stories on SC. It was like July 4th going off in my head, firing off dopamine shocks, leaving my mind feeling like a night sky with no stars, a dark space. The only thing I had after the number of likes was the birth of my anxiety. Since this chapter is asking you, "what's your number?" Do not focus on the numbers above; on top of your social media accounts. Ask yourself, what is the number of hours you spend on your accounts? What is the number of days a week you use social media? What is the number of real friends that you have in your life? How about I give you a number right now?

The number 7; how about seven days, social media free? Begin a seven-day fast for yourself to start. Challenge yourself; figure out who you are again without the validation from random strangers for one week. Now, this is my number one rule; I cannot tell anyone how to live their life. If you are okay with social media, you feel that it does not have the best of you, or you are not addicted to these platforms; by all means, continue with your business. Only you should know what is best for you, as long as you know yourself.

I find it fascinating, numbers I mean. Think about it; these ten digits, "1,2,3,4,5,6,7,8,9 and 0." We use these numbers to represent our height, our weight, our net worth. We exchange cell phone numbers, to stay connected, we use numbers for mathematics, measurements, and science. But even though we use numbers every single day; they should never represent our worth as human beings; never. I would never expect to have a number represent who I am. Those numbers, in a way, are like having a price on us.

The higher the number, the more valuable you are; the more expensive you are. Best believe there is a science behind all of this, a science to keep all of us addicted. Speaking of numbers, I am now going to address the date I escaped this nightmare, the day of August 25th, 2018.

6 *Likes*

August 25th; The Day I Escaped the Nightmare.

I remember it very precisely. The time was five o'clock in the morning, around the time when it is still a little dark outside. The birds were chirping, but my heart was racing as if I saw a ghost. I had one of the worst cases of anxiety that I ever experienced in my life. I sat myself up in my bed; to try to get myself together. But my mind was producing a thousand thoughts a minute. Why was this happening? I was terrified; I had to do something to calm myself down. So, I hopped out of my bed and rushed to the bathroom. I splashed some water on my face and looked at myself in the mirror. Only to find out that I did not see myself when I looked. I saw someone else, another soul that was not mine. I took such a hard look in that mirror.

I could not recognize myself; I did not see me; I did not see Jordan Wells. I saw a bot, an avatar that I helped create for the sake of carrying on this false image of who I thought I wanted to be; for the acceptance of others. This was a nightmare come true. I needed to wake up from it seriously. Freddy Kruger himself could not conduct this nightmare; it was horrible. The light in the bathroom felt as if it was getting brighter and brighter on my face. I almost thought that I was hallucinating, as if I saw things that were not there. Fear and anxiety were hand and hand in my consciousness; I could not hear myself; I could not think properly. I could not even put on a fake smile and pretend everything was alright. It was like the devil had my mind, my soul, and my body. Ready to direct me back to my phone; to plug my brain right back into this nightmare world that I was heavily addicted to since I was sixteen years old.

But I just had to find a way to calm myself down, as the anxiety was starting to go up a few knots. So, I went down to my basement, where I had my treadmill; I walked on there for over an hour and a half. I just walked; I walked and walked some more. I did not have my fingers scrolling on the screen of my smartphone that morning. But my feet were scrolling on the belt of my treadmill. As I walked on my treadmill, I was trying to figure out why I was feeling this way. Why was I feeling overwhelmed and anxious? Where did these chaotic emotions come from so suddenly? I had a severe problem. Something was wrong, and I was scared as hell.

After I got off the treadmill; I showered off the pain a little, dried myself off, and for the second time; I took a long stare in the mirror. That long uncomfortable stare; seeing that guy in the mirror; was an intervention. Divine intervention if you will. To this day, I do not know who that soul was that I was looking at in the mirror. But that soul was giving me the answer that I had was looking for since I was sixteen years old. The answer was simple; I had to cold turkey, delete my social media accounts. I had to break the addictive chains of mental enslavement that were keeping me in this cognitive imprisonment.

As I picked up my phone to take a look and see if there were any notifications; that is when it hit me. The night before that morning, I was on my phone. I was on social media, looking at everyone else's lives, and being self-distracted. In which I truthfully was being self-destructive and not even knowing I was. All night long, I was scrolling up and down my phone, self-hypnotizing my consciousness into this matrix. When I recall that night, I did not fall asleep until three in the morning. I only slept for two hours. My brain was out of control, I was in a panic state of mind, at my lowest point that morning; it was so bad. So, what did I do? I made one final post on Ivory; I did something that represented a cry for help. I posted a selfie with the caption spelled backward. The caption said, "*flesym rof srewnsa yna evah t'nod tsuj I, yawa og ot niap eht lla tnaw tsuj I.*" You may need a few seconds to look at what I said. I did not want just to say it so bluntly. I was in a very vulnerable, depressed mindset that morning. That feeling was horrifying when I think about it now.

So, it was time to escape; time to delete all of this madness and run forward to reality. That is what I did; that was the last day I posted on Ivory; I said goodbye to her forever. Before I deleted Ivory off of my phone, I received a comment under that one last post; from my great friend Tawny. I met Tawny on the set of a Netflix show called "*Russian Doll.*" We both were the stand-ins for the two main actors of the show. She was the stand-in for actress Natasha Lyonne, and I was standing in for actor Charlie Barnett. Tawny was my partner in crime. We had great chemistry working together; overall, a great experience working on that show with everyone. Anyways, she was the only one who reached out to me on social media and gave me comfort. I told Tawny that I was quitting all of the social media, and she did not think that was a bad idea. She understood me and where I was coming from and respectfully supported my decision. I am forever grateful to Tawny for reaching out to me that day, and I love her dearly for that, as well as my best friend Maddy, who I also spoked to that same morning.

So that was it for me; I was done with Ivory, out of my life, just like that. I got rid of all of my old and recent posts, permanently deleted my account, and never looked back. I gave none of my followers any warnings; I did not feel the need to inform anyone. Those of who I was legit friends with, in my personal life, that I knew personally and spent time with; I had other ways of staying in contact with them. So, it was a cold turkey decision.

Twitchell was a no brainer; I never had a use for it. If my professor in college never made opening an account mandatory for the class, I do not believe that I would have ever made an account. I cannot even recall the username I had for Twitchell. The next to go was Mr. Sam Chapman. What was interesting about Sam Chapman; after I disabled my account, if I did not reactivate after several days, my account automatically is deleted. So, it disappeared on its own.

Last but not least; the megalodon, the wizard, the mastermind. The one and only; Franklin Benjamin, or "FB." Now, even though I deleted the apps from my smartphone, I still had my FB account active for several weeks after I deleted everything else. The only reason why I reserved deleting FB; my birthday was coming up, and I knew that on FB; some people would wish me a happy birthday. So, I just kept FB opened until the day after my birthday.

On that day; I made my final FB post, and on that post, I said this exactly;

"First, I would like to just say thank you to everyone who had taken the time to wish me a Happy Birthday yesterday. God has truly blessed me with another year on this Earth; 29! The last year of my 20's. But honestly, this is the first time I have been on Facebook, or any social media, since August. I won't get into details of why, but it came to the point of me basically staying away and quitting all of the social media at once. My mind was telling me I had to make a change in my life, and this is that change. To be honest, I'm sincerely at peace with myself since I've quit social media. I'm barely on my phone. My mind is clear, and I'm more focused than I've ever been. Truthfully, I'm happy and at peace with myself. Scrolling all day long, looking at hundreds, thousands of different people's lives, most of them we'll never even meet. It could be detrimental to our mental health, I would know. So, I decided to take that big step away from these platforms, and it was the best decision I made for MYSELF. I'm not saying that everyone should just quit cold turkey. You may see the light in your own time. To each his own. But I will say that after two days of NOT being on my phone, not on social media, has changed my life. I have my life back, the real one. Not the virtual one. At this point, I have no further purpose of posting things or simply to be on social media anymore. So, this will be my last post. My last time on social media. I already deleted/deactivated everything else. Whoever reads this last post, I would like to

thank you very much, from the bottom of my heart, for showing me so much love and support since day one, through the journey of my acting career, and just me period. That's my ultimate focus. I WILL continue to progress; you will continue to see me winning and living my dream. Just not through this social media world anymore. I wish you all nothing but the best for your lives."

Afterward, some terrific friends and people I had worked with in college reached out to me, wished me well, and how courageous I was for leaving social media behind. I hope they are all doing well.

There you have it; I did what I had to do. But what I found hilarious in deleting my FB account; in the process of removing myself. I was getting layers of different pages, multiple warnings saying, "once you delete your account, you will no longer have access to it." As if they were subliminally seducing me to stay. The repeated emails; unnecessary emails about other people liking post of someone who I was not even following. Notifications and emails from both FB and Ivory, saying, "Hey, your friend just got engage, go congratulate them." "Your friend is on live, go check them out before they go offline." That is when I truly realized that we are being programmed by these things. They want your time, your soul, and your conscience; they want it all.

It reminded me of the last scene in the movie "*The Truman Show*," starring Jim Carrey. I felt like Truman when he was about to walk out of that bubble of a simulated town; full of actors with fake identities. I felt like this entity was trying to prevent me from escaping; manipulating me with those emails, trying to get me to stay in the social media world. But I chose to say goodbye, and I stepped back into reality.

I knew what time it was; it was time to get the hell away from all of these platforms. In my mind, in my spirit, I had to escape. I hid from the notifications by deleting the apps from my phone. I could no longer be seduced by those machines anymore. I could not be lured in, consciously because I did not see it. I did not see anything that anyone was doing with their lives. I protected my eyes, my mind, and, most importantly, my precious time.

I admit I was thinking about all of what I could potentially miss out on—staying up to date with college friends, engagements, friends having kids, and all the good things that were real. Maybe even to find a potential lover of my own. But at what cost, though? I did not want my life, being consumed by four separate apps, constantly battling for my time. It made no sense to me; none of it did. It was just an "*artificial addiction*," as Jaron Lanier once described it in an interview. I was miserable with it all. This social media world was not living to me. It was living lies, fantasies, dreams that did not come true yet. No more for me, though. No more taking real friendships and reducing them to "likes." No more followers or following other people, no one could unfollow me, block me, or delete me as a friend ever again. I just focused on following my dreams. I went my own way.

I felt that I was moving on to a new life. I felt like a boy that became a new man. I no longer had to post myself doing something or saying something that needed instant feedback: instant comments, frequent, and constant attention. I was no longer putting my mind through cognitive destruction, and in return, I gained cognitive salvation. Salvation is in my life now. I was safe from intellectual brutality. Sheltered from the soul-sucking virtual machines that give us likes, in exchange for our precious time out of our precious lives.

Even though August 25th starting so horribly for me, it ended so peacefully. I was able to find peace, as I said in my final FB post. I also reconnected with my soul. I realized that I lost my soul, not just in social media, but in the time I wasted for twelve years. From the ages sixteen to twenty-eight; I did not take a break from social media. I honestly believe, had I not logged off of social media, I would have traded my soul, little by little, solely for likes, views, and followers. The bottom line is that I had to escape; I did survive, and it was about damn time.

7 *Likes*

I Have Time for You Now

I believe that time is a disease, but it is a delicate disease. Every living breathing being on this earth has this disease. Time deteriorates our bodies; it is a disease that is irreversible. From the day we are born, we are infected, until the day we leave here. However, time is the one disease that we would love to have forever. Unfortunately, there is a cure for this disease. We call it death. The reason I call time a disease is because, like many other diseases, we do not get to choose whether we want to have it or not. We did not ask for it, we do not know where time comes from, and we did not ask to be born; it just is what it is. Also, we do not know how much time we become infected with on this earth. Time changes us through our growth, our knowledge, self-knowledge, and preparation in this hospital that we call life. So, why do we, human beings, waste so much of our delicate time on these social media apps? I spent much of my precious time on this earth; scrolling, and scrolling, and scrolling. Just to see images of everyone else, living a life that they may not even be living truthfully. We spend hours upon hours a day on these platforms with our heads down in another world. I mean, why people? How did we make it so?

The first few days when I escaped, I had so much time on my hands. I did not know what to do with myself. This freedom I felt, for the first time in twelve years that I was not using social media at all. But what was I going to do now? I gave it some thought, and I finally did something that knocked down the concrete walls surrounding my brain and released my cognitive abilities. I picked up a book.

Well, now that I recall, it was not that simple. I did not pick up a book for about three weeks after I deleted my accounts. I needed some time to heal, mentally. I made some time for myself. I used that time to wake up from that nightmare that I had been sleeping in, for those twelve years. I was in recovery time; I begin to watch some videos on the topic of "quitting social media." As I watched some videos, I started to feel that there was some support in my decision. I begin to understand that I was not alone. Then I came across a man by the name of Jaron Lanier, who I mentioned earlier.

I remembered the thumbnail photo of Jaron; he had on black glasses and had these long brown dreadlocks that stretched almost down to the floor. I could just tell he's lived life and experienced some utopian things. It was an interview of Jaron on the talk show "The View." So, I made time for this man to hear what he had to say about this subject. I opened the video that ran for about six minutes or so. Jaron was promoting his new book, *"Ten Arguments for Deleting Your Social Media Accounts Right Now."* Jaron talked about the dangers of social media and how it is affecting our behavior, our minds, and how it is ruining our lives.

At that moment, in that interview, Jaron was like my doctor. He was telling me through the television screen, all the symptoms I had leading to my addiction to social media. I knew very little about how there is a third party involved in this "*manipulation machine*," as Lanier phrased it. There was so much that I did not understand that I do now; after watching that video. Jaron said something that stuck with me. He said, *"The other thing I want to say is; young people, the greatest gift that you can have for yourself is self-knowledge, and until you can at least experience life outside of the manipulation machine, you can't know yourself as well."* Jaron Lanier could not have said that any better for me to understand. I needed to hear that more than ever. After watching that one interview of Lanier, I begin to do more research on him. I saw that Jaron had other accomplishments, one being a pioneer of virtual reality, a musician, and a computer scientist.

I went to purchase his book. I stopped at a bookstore in Columbus Circle. His book was the first book I read after I escaped the social media world. His book was all the support that I needed. It was a page-turner; Jaron enlightened me with a lot of his philosophy on life and how beautiful it can be without social media. One thing Jaron was sincere about in his book and his interviews was that he refused to demonize or vilify the people who work at these tech companies, or technology period. I can respect that, as well.

I learned a lot from this man, Jaron Lanier. I consider him a huge supporter of my decision to leave and abandon these social media platforms. I thank him, and I am forever grateful for his book and message. I also thank two others as well; Cal Newport and Tristan Harris. For me, after listening to Cal Newport's presentation. I felt his perspective on social media showed that I no longer needed social media to enhance or elevate my acting career. I do not need social media to stay relevant, nor do I need these platforms to help keep me motivated in life. Tristan Harris is one who talks about how these "smartphones" are designed to keep us addicted. All of those notifications ringing every two minutes, the constant checking of our phones.

I believe all three of these men can concur that these smartphones and social media together are nothing more but slot machines. I ultimately agreed and understood that logic. I followed and understood that analogy; based on my own experiences with both smartphones and an actual slot machine. Instead of sliding in money into a slot machine and pulling the handle, I was putting in my valuable time to pay the social media machine. Social media are the games; smartphones are the actual slot machines, and posting was the handle to gamble. With both logics, I realized how much money and time I wasted in my life, how I could have used both of my time and money on much more productive things. I guess you can say I lost big on these gambles. It is funny how they give you just enough winnings to make you stay and continue to play. Making you feel that you are just warming up the machine. One makes you think that you are going to hit the jackpot, the other makes you think that you are going to go viral.

In some cases, that actually can happen, but they are rare. The reality is, the house always wins. These machines, the slot machines, social media, and smartphones, are deliberately designed to keep you addicted, period! I was convinced; I had all the support I needed from Jaron, Cal, and Tristan. I made my decision final and permanent. As long as I live, never to waste my precious time living a false imaged life on social media.

After I finished reading Jaron Lanier's book, I was looking forward to another. The next book I took the time to read was, "*The Autobiography of Joseph Stalin.*" I know, an unexpected choice, right? I heard about Stalin from an old interview of the late great hip hop legend, Tupac Amaru Shakur. Tupac mentioned in the discussion, how he was an avid reader, since a very young age. I have no idea how many books Tupac read, but he inspired me to read, and I was willing to commit to reading multiple books myself. So, in the interview, he begins to name some of the books he was currently reading at the time. He mentioned that he was reading a book about Joseph Stalin. Before that time, I never heard of Stalin. I guess the name "Joseph Stalin" alone, had some kind of charisma. So, that was the next book I read. I coincidently already had the book about Stalin in my home. There was a shelf of free books when I was in college, so I helped myself to them.

I will just say this; after reading Joseph Stalin's autobiography, it opened my mind up to a completely different view of people and the world we live in today. What I learned is that no one is born entirely evil. It is a choice to walk an evil path in life. There is that saying, "that it takes a village to raise a child." I say, "It takes a village to create a monster." Since his childhood, Stalin was not a stranger to violence. Could you even imagine; if Stalin and Hitler got their hands on to social media? What would they tweet? Executions? Live on people's social media accounts? The holocaust, the murders, and all the other evil acts that took place at that time.

That book, about that man, taught me that power is the number one drug of choice; that any man, woman, or child would kill to have, literally. If you have power and control in this world, you can do anything. The harsh reality is some people would choose to do evil in the world rather than good. It is as if every so often, people with power feel that they are God. When in reality, they are just vulnerable, insecure human beings, living in fear that is protected by ego. Some people have wealth in money and become a philanthropist. Other people are wealthy in fear and become a philanthropist of fear, anxiety, and also pain.

To be honest; I was not an avid reader of books before I quit social media. When I was in school, I did my homework, of course, and did my research when needed. Still, my attention span and interest in reading books were no match for my social media addiction. As long as I stayed on my accounts, I would be "misinformed" of all the news of today. I would never be out of the loop, as long as I stayed online. But I was naïve; I was ignorant and wasted so much time. No, I cannot get that time back, but for whatever time I have left, I can make things right. Which leads me to the third book I read, "*The Machine Stops*," by E.M. Forster.

I learned about this book from Jaron Lanier, who, in an interview, asked the audience if they read this book. In disbelief, none of the audience members raised their hands.

So, Jaron went on to discuss this book, which made me interested enough to make that the next book I looked forward to reading. What I learned from this book is that people really can predict the future. In the book, there are two main characters; the mother and her son Kuno. By the way, author E.M. Forster wrote this book around the year 1909-1910. In "*The Machine Stops*," Forster wrote, *"But it was fully fifteen seconds before the round plate that she held in her hands began to glow. A faint blue light shot across it, darkening to purple, and presently she could see the image of her son, who lived on the other side of the earth, and he could see her."* Now, does that sound familiar to you? Is that not what we are doing in our world today? Glowing plates where we can interact with each other; see each other from different locations around the globe. We have Skype, Facetime, What's App, our smartphones, tablets, laptops, and computers. All of which have webcams to connect us in a visual format.

Even though this is a book, E.M. Forster was pretty spot on with his vision of a world where a machine controls everything. But the one thing that Forster also mentioned in his book is how this machine crashes. The outrage caused to the people; and how so many were entirely reliant on this computer machine, that they could not survive without it. Thus, a lot of people died underground. While others managed to escape, reached the surface of the earth, and saw the Sun for the first time in years. It is a fantastic book; one I recommend reading. After reading "*The Machine Stops*," I went on to read "*The Power of the Actor,*" by Ivana Chubbuck, "*The Time Machine*," by H.G. Wells, and several others. I was proud of myself. I took my precious time and found a focus in literature again.

My mind was becoming more focused on myself after my social media departure. I was reading, and I was working out almost every day. I just had so much time for myself now. It was life-changing for me—a life with no social media. I remembered after the first week of quitting all of it; I took a trip to New York City. I was listening to music on the train and came across this song called "*It Feels Like Summer*" by Childish Gambino. It is a beautiful song, uplifting lyrics. As I was walking down the streets, I was just looking around. I was looking at the streets of Manhattan, looking at the people all over. I felt so refreshed with not checking my phone every two minutes. I was not checking for notifications. I felt like a new man, observing a new world. That song just allowed me to reflect. Reflect on myself and my life. I realized that I did not know much about myself at all. I knew what I wanted to do with my life but did not entirely understand who I was as a person. That was not so clear to me. Spending so many years on those platforms, I practically lost my identity. I knew that I had a lot of work to do from that point on.

Time; what is time? Is time just a made-up compass, that we use for direction in our lives? Is time some kind of artificial intelligence that controls our purpose of what we do with our lives and how we do it? Perhaps "time" is like what I believe it to be; a delicate disease that we would love to have forever. But we cannot have it forever, which is why I say to myself so many times in my life. "If I only knew then what I know now." I probably would not have started this whole nightmare. Regrets are the symptoms of the disease of time. But there are other things besides "time" that has changed in my life. Time was just the luxury that I needed to heal and better myself. The other thing that I reflect on was my beliefs. My feelings of a higher power. A higher consciousness, and the actual views of living in a better world. My passions in changing the world are not dead. I believe the world could change, but we have to start changing ourselves one day at a time. I made the changes that worked best for me. I made the smart, necessary choices to change myself; to contribute to the journey in changing the world.

I chose to stop consuming meat, chicken, turkey, and pork. I have not indulged in over eight years. Now I continue this lifestyle by removing seafood and all dairy as well. Some will call that being a vegan. I just call it changing my life, for the better, of not only myself but the environment. Choices are crucial in our lives. Choices in what we eat and how much we eat; can increase or decrease the time we have on this earth. So, I made these choices to change who I am. To remove the bad habits that I was comfortable with sustaining in my everyday life. My motto with all of this is simple; "If you want to be a better person, just take the actions necessary to be a better person." Of course, it is a challenge. It is a good challenge to have. I have to admit, though; giving up dairy was the challenge from hell. The cheese was my drug of choice. I would never turn down pizza. But I somehow made that sacrifice, and I made that choice to remove it all. Cheese, milk, eggs, and I hardly drink coffee anymore. I know; coffee! How did I go on with my life every day without coffee? Well, I use these things called courage and, of course, time. I do not know how I live this lifestyle every day; to make that full commitment. However, to be clear and to be understood about all of this. I did what was best for me.

I said this earlier; I cannot and will not tell anyone what to do with their own life. Learn your lessons, make wise choices for yourself, and take your time. One of my favorite songs from the rock band "Talk Talk," "*Life's what you make it*," is what I go by as far a living life. I happen to believe, metaphorically speaking, that we are all songs. All seven-plus billion of us are songs, with our original lyrics that tell our stories. Some songs last longer than others, but it is really about what you have to say to the world, with your song. If we as people continue allowing these social media platforms to linger on with the manipulation, the fake news, the hunger, and seduction for attention. Likes, comments, views, and followers. If we do not make personal changes, we will be living the same song, lyrics, tunes, and running off the same frequencies, with absolutely no originality. We would just be a bunch of copycats and pirates.

Only time will tell what is to come in the future. I have my thoughts about what will be next. I believe that social media will not go anywhere, and neither will smartphones. However, I hope for a better tomorrow, a better future for the next generation. Hope is a muscle we must train. To the young people who are reading this book right now, *"I spent and wasted a lot of time out of my youth on these social media apps. I cannot get that time back. It is gone forever, and nothing from these apps have contributed to making my life better. Now that is not to say that you will have the same experiences on social media as I did. If all is well on your part, then many blessings. However, you should never feel obligated to have an account, just for the sake of keeping up with the party and getting with the program. Do not dedicate too much of your precious time on these platforms. Enjoy your lives by being in the moment. I know you do not want to suffer from "FOMO," "Fear of Missing Out."*

But I fear for you; I fear that you will miss out on your own life, being distracted and giving so much of your time to social media and smartphones. Remember this; you do not owe anyone an image of your success, your love life, or your happiness. Sometimes when life is treating you great, just put a smile on your face and enjoy it at that moment. Find your moment; find the right time for you to realize that you are wasting much time on virtual validation. I hope you will understand what I am saying someday. I believe you will, and I have faith a change will come to where you will no longer allow social media to define you." Only time will tell this tale.

8 *Likes*

A Year Later

My God, if only you knew how I feel today. It has been over a year since I logged off, over a year since I escaped that nightmare. If I could compare it to heaven on earth, I would. That is what it feels like for me. It feels like mental emancipation. Let me tell you; every day of the first week I quit social media; I walked out of my house, I looked up to the sky and gazed at that summer sun. Not looking down at my phone all day long, since I was no longer active on any social media, I was able to lift my head, look up, and see the sun. It was like I saw the sun for the first time in twelve years. Similar to E.M. Forster's book that I mentioned earlier, about how the people underground came up to the surface of the earth and saw the sun for the first time in years. Just like the song from that children's show, "*Barney*," I let the sunshine down on me. For the first time in the twelve years, I felt a much better light. Natural Vitamin-D light was shining on my face; instead of that artificial blue light glowing on my face from a laptop, tablet, smartphone, or television. The sun was the light that I was finally able to see. I looked up at the ocean blue sky, closed my eyes, and breathed. I breathed in and out with no distractions. My neck even had to adjust to the difference. Being that I was no longer positioning my neck, looking down at a phone all day, developing what is called the "text neck."

I talked about how much free time I had, now I have to elaborate on how I just felt after a year. I felt like I was that sixteen-year-old kid again; before I even opened up a Myspace account. Innocent; fresh from any manipulation. I wish I could have told the sixteen-year-old version of myself, "*Do not use these things! Do not waste your life away. Do not give your soul and precious time away for irrelevant validation.*" But now, I have put all that foolishness in the past. I escaped this nightmare and became the man that I choose to be. This journey has been a feeling of being reborn. I can now lift my head and observe the reality. I can be in the moment, see life for what it is, and without the manipulation or opinions of others.

I could feel the hard shell of distraction in my mind began to crack like Humpty Dumpty. No social media notifications, none of the constant vibrations, no more updated status hitting my smartphone. I was free! Free from the images of everyone else's lives. All of the celebrities, families, and friends. Not knowing what is going on in other people's lives is not so bad, to be honest with you. After I was off of social media for over a year, I would run into friends and people I was friends with on social media, and they would ask me, "where did you go? Haven't seen you in a while." That felt great because I could then ask them genuinely, "How are you?" Asking them that question without seeing them online, felt more like a real question and that I could get a real answer.

To see what people are doing on social media, and then you see them in real-time. You ask the same question, already knowing the answer because you have seen their presence online. The responses would be predictable. You know I must say this as well, the healthiest thing you can do is to mind your own business. That is the smartest, healthiest thing you can do. You get so much done in your own life. You find your purposes, your passions, your place in this world when you mind your business. It is complicated when you have access to all of these other people's lives: their accomplishments, downfalls, and depression. Once I logged off, I knew that was it. That would be the last time I see a lot of the people from my social media accounts, but that was okay for me. It is okay that you do not know what is going on with everyone else day by day. Vice versa, people do not have to know what is going on with your life daily.

People were not real to me online. I felt that everyone was just avatars and bots. My care for people had declined. People were becoming one dimensional to me, from only seeing them online. Social media programs you to see people only as numbers, that is why it is so easy to unfollow and block people. Even your friends and family. Again, people are strange.

It is so funny now; when I interact with people today; and have conversations with them, people always ask me, "what is your social media?" When I tell them, I am no longer on social media; they look at me like I am E.T. They see me as if I am not of this world. People would say to me, "You need it; how do you expect to make connections or get to know people?" Let me just tell you this; I mentioned before that I am an actor. I have now been a member of SAG-AFTRA for over three years. From the ages of twenty-one to twenty-eight, I have not received one job or audition from this industry; via social media. These platforms are now simply meant for "show and tell." Show your business; tell your business.

Social media has not helped my acting career in no way shape or form. Now I cannot speak for anyone else. I am sure that many people have made it big by going viral. That is great for them. However, it is the luck of the slot machine. People get lucky and hit the jackpot, but it is very few who do. Besides, the things I have seen people do to go viral are just not of moral principles. The day I see an actor or actress accept an Academy Award and give thanks to social media for making them a star. I will then take it a little seriously. But I still would not log back on.

Life has been so different since I logged off. I talk differently, I walk differently, especially since I am no longer walking with my head down; hypnotized by my phone. I even listen differently and think differently. When I have conversations with people now, I just listen to what people have to say. Not concerned about agreeing or disagreeing with what the discussion is, but I simply just hear people out. I believe that because of social media, people young and old; are losing their ability to think and listen. I see this a lot with the youth of society. Younger people are losing their cognitive skills, and their attention span is deteriorating. It is too early to obtain any evidence that social media is causing us a great source of depression, anxiety, and addiction. But in my case, I would believe that to be true.

I want to be very clear; I do not portray myself as the victim. I took my free will, and it just got the best of me. I do not blame or rule the CEOs of these social media companies as the villains. It would be as if a professional American football player running a play, gets brutally hit; that leaves him permanently paralyzed from the waist down. Should that player then blame the founder of American Football? No, it is just the unfortunate cards he was dealt in the game of life. As I said, I was a young, naïve sixteen-year-old kid when I started, and I became addicted. I barely had a life to live at that time and did not know what I was getting myself into with these platforms. I am not anti-smartphones, nor am I entirely anti-social media. I am an anti-addiction personality. I do not believe that any addictions deliver sincerity to our lives. Too much of anything is good for absolutely nothing.

There are only four ways I stay in touch with people now. That is a phone call, text message, emails, or just meeting people in person. Some of you may say that I am just keeping it old school. I would not call this old school, but a better school, or maybe even real school. These are the most efficient ways for me to stay in contact with people. It is more direct and personal.

Life without these platforms so far has been very liberating, and I would even say necessary. The thing is I know that I cannot just expect people to cold turkey quit and delete their accounts. That is not my primary purpose for why I wrote this book. My main goal is to present you with a different option. To give you a different perspective on how you can live your life. To show you what life is like, on the other side of the fence. Not being on social media, I no longer feel obligated to disclose anything that goes on in my life in exchange for views and likes. Having a private life is a healthier life, a life of happiness. Do not worry about missing out on anything. When you see something on social media, something horrifying, but you cannot do anything at that moment. You cannot prevent it, you cannot stop it, nor can you change the outcome. Then from that grows anger inside of you. But the only thing you can do about it at that moment; is to repost that incident and express how you feel about it, and the only results you see are views, likes, and comments. Then what is next? Eighty percent of what goes on via social media has nothing to do with you or your life. You are not missing out on random strangers who you will never even know or see in life. All these new movements now, and you do not have to even move out of your chair. Just post about it; with hashtags.

Please remember this; the best friend you will ever have in this life is tomorrow. You can have millions of dollars, multiple cars, multiple friends that you hang out with, but if you do not have tomorrow, you have nothing. So, logging off of social media is not a loss, but it is your gain. The choice is always up to you, of course. I just wanted to present that to you, especially the younger generations that are moving forward. Again, you do not owe anyone an image of your success, or even your troubled times.

I became a better person. I am not bitter; about the world or life. I finally know what it feels like to have happiness in my life. I wonder if happiness is something we can only feel. Is happiness an experience or something we actually can have? I happen to believe that happiness is not necessarily just a feeling, but somewhat of an experience. The reason I say that is this; let's say, for example, I am a billionaire.

Every night I go to bed; I know in my mind that there are people who are living in poverty, homeless, sleeping out on the streets with children and babies in the cold. How could I be happy with billions of dollars, knowing that there are homeless people out there? For me to experience happiness, I would have to do something about those homeless people. I would use my financial means to help, to make a difference, and if I were to save some of the homeless, that would be the experience, and that would be my happiness. I do not believe having tons of money brings joy and happiness. I do not think having a garage of ten luxurious cars brings you happiness. It would bring an overwhelming state of mind.

Happiness is of good experiences we go through in our lives. I do not believe happiness is something we can just feel all day long. As I said early about scrolling up and down on social media, going from happy to sad, and then laughing in a matter of seconds. I remember a time when someone asked me, "are you happy?" I had to think about it, and I realized I was not. I did not know what happiness was at that time. I did not know if I was supposed to be happy or feel happy. To think about what happiness is, made me think of sadness.

My take on this is that happiness and sadness are experiences and not a state of being. The experience of happiness is what you could do, not just for yourself, but for others. The experience of sadness is believing you deserve more or want more, yet you have more than others. Still, you do not have use or value for what you already possess. Which then leaves you overwhelmed and depressed. I do not believe that you should hold people responsible for your happiness or your sadness. Both are your sole responsibility.

I am still in the practice of that. You should not go through life thinking people owe you something, just because you met them once or have had a conversation.

I tie this into my social media experience. I held people responsible for my happiness and my sadness. I believed that as I received a lot of likes and followers, I was special; I thought that was happiness. But as I said, the more likes I received, the unhappier I became. Which then led to sadness—the sadness of not hearing back from the people that I messaged—then trying to make them feel a little guilty for not responding.

Having all four of these platforms and not knowing how to use them properly, I ended up being used by these addictive machines. I Learned that happiness and sadness are in our own hands. Only you can decide whether or not you want to experience happiness or sadness. We will experience both in life; because life is not always fair or something we can adequately prepare for as imperfect humans. So, when you experience sadness, be in the moment of that as well. Live through it, learn from it, and know that it is just a moment in time that will not defeat you.

I say this to say, if you were to quit social media, your life is not just going to become perfect or worry-less. But I guarantee you; you will feel liberated from artificial validation. You will have more focus on your own life and your dreams, and whatever you go through, you will not feel the pressure to share your business on a platform, to be judged.

I live a life of no judgment. I understand people come from different paths of life and who went through things that I may have never experienced. I see that now. I know that what is best for me may not be what is best for everyone else. Also, I see myself being less defensive and being able to handle things with class, to handle situations as an adult. I guess I can say, for the first time in my life, after I logged off, I was able to know so much more about myself because I was focused solely on myself. I know who I am now as a person, as a man. I realized that I am not perfect, and that is perfectly okay with me.

I do not have to put on a facade that shows this amazingly perfect life of an actor. I became a human being again. I was not trying to prove anything to anyone. I was able to see better, think better, and love for real. Food tasted better than ever before. I know you may be thinking, "what does food tasting better have to do with social media?" Well, for me, I have been off of social media for over a year, and that made me feel better mentally. So, I took the next level and went on an entirely plant-based diet. Even thou I stopped eating red meat, chicken, turkey, and pork years ago, I sealed the deal by letting go of seafood and dairy, as I mentioned before. But let me just say; that is for a whole other book, and I am no expert on dieting. A plant-based diet has been working for me and I am only speaking for myself on that subject. It would not hurt to try though.

A year after I quit social media, I was no longer a hoodwinked person, falling into the fake news and click-baiting traps that produce lies within it. Politics in this country has become a crying joke; not tears of laughter, but tears of panic and chaos. I do not even like using the word politics anymore; I call it "politicks."

Paranoia invading the minds of millions, and I believe society is conditioning the minds of the masses to regret the future and prepare for the past. Twitchell has become the adopted parent to politicians. Talk show host having their debates. "I disagree with this; I disagree with that." Co-host cutting each other off in mid-sentence, discussing politics. Conservatives at war with liberals. Who is the cat, who is the underdog? Can't we all just get along, right? I guess we will not succeed in getting along together in this life right now.

I am not stopping at a year; in fact, I have no desire to go back on social media, ever. I have taken all the selfies I could take. I have seen all that I needed to see that these products had to offer. Those numbers do not define me; I define me. I have my own life now. I have a life of self-worth, self-respect, self-knowledge, self-acceptance, self-validation, and, most importantly, self-love. Life is quite beautiful without social media; let me tell you. Life became real for me again. I realized that I got away from it all, not just for the right reasons, but also at the right time. At an age where I am still a young man in developing who I am, where I want to be, and how I am going to get there. Some people may think; because I do not eat meat, I do not drink, do not smoke, and have no social media whatsoever; that I have completely lost it; I lost my mind. But the way I feel about it is this; society has lost my mind. This society that once controlled my mind has now lost my mind. I then found my mind, cleansed, and squeezed out the toxins and contaminations that society has soaked into it, and now I finally have a mind of my own.

9 *Likes*

Save The Children

I think of a song that was made by the late great Marvin Gaye. A song called "*Save the Children*" from his album "*What's Going On*?" It is one of the most beautiful albums I ever heard and one of the most beautiful songs ever made. Marvin had something to say on that album. If you have not listened to this song before, please do when you can. I believe what has happened to the world today; is an echo of what Marvin was singing about in that record, some forty-eight years ago. I cannot help but wonder what impact all of this social media is doing to the minds of the children, not just in America, but all over the world. As well as the excessive use of smartphones that these kids are now devotedly engaged with every day. What are these kids gaining from being exposed to the madness and confusion of society? Between social media, drug addiction, alcohol, sex, vaping, and God knows what else there is to come. Now that I am not looking at a screen all day long, I noticed the young ones are hooked on their screens more than anyone. Two eyes, two thumbs, a naïve brain, and time are the main ingredients for this digital metamorphosis. Those are all the resources these platforms need to keep us addicted. I see that kids are having a hard time trying to break this habit, and some adults as well. I feel for the generations that will come after me. They are born into this social media world, born to be addicted.

What I saw during my college years was just the beginning of what I see today in the younger generation. As I said earlier, I would see infants using these smartphones. A baby would drop their bottle multiple times, but it is something about these smartphones that they hold on to for dear life with the tightest grip. Their fresh eyes are gazing at those multi-pixel screens, all the different colors, better than any toy they ever played with, in their playpen. Smartphones have become the new babysitter. Babies are born on social media. People are recording videos of a mother while she is giving birth, for their profiles on Ivory, FB, Sam Chapman, and YouTube. Memories to cherish, we see these babies growing up on these channels. I wonder if they will ever get a chance to know themselves, as a person, as a human being.

I still remember my childhood. I had toys to play with; wrestling action figures, Tonka trucks, power rangers, some video games, and VHS tapes of my favorite childhood movies. Every Friday I would go to the video store and rent movies with my family. Today, I cannot recall the last time I saw a video store in ten years. Today, these kids with these electronics and virtual services. Social media, Netflix, YouTube, smartphones, tablets, laptops, and computers. Nothing that requires them to break a sweat or to use their minds to think. It is cognitively unhealthy for these kids. I believe that society has overwhelmed the youth with options. It has programmed them into believing that everything in life is optional.

In reality, some things are not negotiable. Do what you have to do. It seems that the younger generations feel the need to lie their way out of trouble, out of difficult situations, and then play the victim. That is another thing as well; people, young and old, are being conditioned, programmed to be a victim. Not to say that people are not truthfully being mistreated or harmed. However, the effect that social media is having on our society; being a victim is the new superhero. The new icon so to speak. The attention that is given to people when they are telling abusive childhood stories or sexual assault stories, drug addiction, and bullying, which are significant issues in America. They are compelling subjects that the public is desperately infatuated with exploiting. What concerns me about these vulnerable stories is this; People, young people, will believe they can solve their problems, only through social media. To share their traumatizing experiences before seeking help from people in their personal lives. People in their families, close friends, or for God's sake, a therapist. I must say this though; if you are or have ever been a victim of any abuse, do not wait to get help. Do not reserve your abuse! No matter how afraid you are to disclose such a traumatic experience. You never know, you could prevent someone else becoming a victim.

I see celebrities come out of the woodworks and talk about their experience with childhood abuse. When I hear about those stories, I ask myself, "Did they speak with a therapist first, before deciding to disclose that personal information with the world?" One thing I have learned about depression, devastation, and vulnerability is this; they are contagious. The more depressing stories people scroll up and down to see, the more depressed people will become. Social media is not a place of comfort or salvation. It is a place of judgment, cyber wars, and fake news for endless views. It is a place that could be beautiful but shows more of darkness. A darkness that some people try to bring light to, but negativity is the mastermind on these platforms.

To be a victim is to be exceptional in today's world. Again, I am fully aware that there are real victims that suffered through real, horrifying life experiences. How the game is opportunistically structured in the social media world, people will choose to play the role of a victim and use victimization as a weapon to attack others. To create a false tale and to play a victim is what I call a profitable trend. I believe that society is generating a generation of children to think that; if you cannot pursue your dreams, be a victim of your dreams.

Where our society is going with this trend, I do not know. However, I believe we all go through forms of victimizing; child abuse, sexual abuse, child molestation, bullying, or obesity, and many others. I hope and pray that the youth will eventually be strong enough to survive the unexpected curveballs that life throws at them. I did not prepare myself all the time when my life was disappointing. But I made a choice not to become a victim. I chose to fight through the bullying in school, fight through the hard times, and when life threw those curveballs, I still took a swing at them. I will continue to keep swinging. That is the key; when life throws those curveballs of victimization, swing away. Whether you hit or miss, what is essential is that you choose to swing through it. What I hope the younger generations get from me is this; protect your dreams. Protect your blessings from the judgmental, envious platforms that social media has grown to become. Your personal lives are yours to cherish. You do not owe any explanations about what you do with your life. Eventually, we will grow tired of keeping the public up to date on our adventures, our careers, our lives in general. Social media has programmed us to think that success comes into our lives so consistently. For example, if a young person just bought a new car, and received over three hundred likes, the most he or she ever had on social media. At first, it is exciting, but after the likes and comments fade, the only thing that may top that is getting a new apartment or a new house. In reality, it takes time for those kinds of achievements, something social media was not technically designed to understand. But people chose to get with the program of social media, and to get with the program; you must be programmed.

Yes, it will be challenging for the kids to break free of these machines; to break free of this road of cyber victimization. Some may think I am overreacting, but am I? Some people may say that "just because I was addicted, does not mean that will happen to me." That is true, but how many drug addicts said the same thing before they took their first hit? Their first shot? I will just say this; I did not have a large following. I only had several hundreds of followers. I was nowhere near hundreds of thousands or millions of followers. You may think, "how was I addicted to social media if I did not even have a large following?" Well, lets' say there are two cocaine addicts. One addict has bricks of cocaine piled up on his desk like he is Tony Montana. Then you have the other addict who only has a gram of cocaine in his possession. Regardless of who has the most cocaine, they are both drug addicts. They are equally dealing with the same disease. So, it does not matter who has a large following or a small one; no one has an addiction that is greater than the next person. It is about who is strong enough to give it all up.

The thing is, I was also a young kid once. I am part of that young generation. I was a young kid with a naïve mentality. I did not know much about addiction; I did not realize I was addicted to social media until I stopped. Many addicts do not know how addicted they are to something until they stop what they are addicted to and reflect on it. As adults, we try our absolute best to reach through to these kids and save them from what we already went through. It is tragically amazing how addictive these drugs are, I must say. A parent who tries to protect their child from drug addiction, the relationship over the years begins to deteriorate. It could be a father and son relationship. The son heavily addicted to drugs, and then over the years, the relationship goes from father and son; to merely just human to human. These drugs are so powerful; that no matter the relationship you have together, you cannot save them based on the love you have for them. I just hope that when the time comes for me to be a father, the world will be more human-friendly. The way society is now, we as people are heading down a dangerous road. It seems as if we always had this problem. A trail of confusion; a path of unwanted destinies, and a road of much-needed attention, that some people would be willing to swerve on and crash, just to get that attention.

So, when I am saying "save the children," I am saying that children are our future innovators. They are the delicate offspring that will bring forth a new world. Hopefully, we will live in a world of healthy living. In a society of less judgment, and proper communication among ourselves. To have a world where the toxic systems of racism and hate are dismantled, replaced with acknowledgment and respect of our differences, in how we live our lives. Then to finally live a life of human civil equality, and children can reach their farthest potentials.

To the children of the future, *"you will change the world. You will bring forth new ways of technology that will eventually cleanse the toxins that have corrupted the platforms of social media. You will find peace with reality, your peace with God, and, most importantly, find and make peace with yourselves. You must take care of yourselves, fourth dimensionally speaking. Take care of yourselves mentally, physically, spiritually, and in-depth—the meaning in detail; what you put into your body. The way your body look on the outside is not half as important as how you should look within. You are living in a world now, where you see yourselves as a business, numbers, a brand, more than you see yourselves as human beings. You have to be human before you try to be anything else. Being that I am no longer on social media, I cannot offer you likes on your post, comments, views, a follow, or friend request. But what I can provide you with, right here by you reading this, is a real warning. Too much social media can put you in a situation that I once trapped myself in for so many years. Deeply depressed, unhappy, addicted, and ultimately lost with no one around to help me. I do not want any of this for you. Regardless of your nationality, ethnicity, sexual orientation, religion, or financial status, these platforms can and will get to you. These machines will make you so bitter, and they will make you hate life and everything in it. I pray you find a way out of this cycle of oblivion. No, I will offer you a solution right now. Isolate yourselves from your accounts as soon as possible. Start first with deleting the apps from your smartphone. That way, you are at least breaking the constant routine of checking your phone every thirty seconds. If you do run a business and market your business via social media, Direct your clients to your company's websites and emails. Emails are still relevant in the business world. As I said before, you do not owe anyone an image of your success.*

Most importantly, with all of that said, you are here for a reason, but you do not have forever on this earth. Do not waste your precious, delicate time away. You are scrolling your thumbs up and down these screens. That will do nothing for you except raise your anxiety, increase your depression, decrease your self-esteem, and finally turn you into an enemy of yourselves. This epidemic is not your fault! You were not aware of the dangers, the consequences that come with these platforms. It is not too late for you. Be bright, brighter than I ever shined. Be wise, beyond your wildest dreams. Be beautiful; more beautiful than a "like" ever falsely validates you to be. Last but certainly not least, be careful."

Life is not perfect; some of you young men and women may not truly hear me right now. But that is fine; everyone will not get it right away; it will take time for some. For example, some nights, you can see the moon, right? It looks as if it is so close to us sometimes, right? But in reality, the moon is approximately 238, 855 miles away from the earth. If we were to walk that distance, it would take close to a decade to get to the moon. That is what I want to relate to you about listening and hearing to what I am saying to you. That someone could be as close to you, right in your face, or even whispering in your ear, warning you of the dangers to come, and it may take you years before you can hear what was said, and understand it. I mean, hey; it took me twelve years before I listened to my intuition. To divine intervention, and I did not have anyone telling me to escape this nightmare. I do not know if you ever heard of Jim Morrison. As I said earlier, Jim is one of my favorite poets; he was the lead singer of a rock band called "The Doors." I remember hearing Jim's voice; in a movie based on The Doors called "*When You're Strange*," directed by Tom DiCillo.

In the movie trailer, you can hear Jim screaming out the words, "*wake up*!" The way Jim screamed it out is the way I wish you can listen to it. "WAKE UP!" Jim screamed it with such sincerity and conviction. As if Jim was trying to create an echo that reached to the farthest ends of the universe. It took me twelve years to wake up. Please do not let it take you that long to wake up from these time-guzzling machines. Do not waste time trying to find friends and love on social media. Focus on finding yourself in society, finding yourself in this world.

Again, I am not here to tell you what to do with your life. I am not in any position to tell anyone how to live. But what I can do is present to you, the younger generations, another alternative. Present to you a different perspective of how your life can be much more meaningful. Life is not always about business, marketing, and success. Life is about being in the moment, embracing your existence on this earth. Knowing how to break free and be still; be quiet.

How can anyone listen to what anyone has to say, when everyone is saying something all at once? What social media has started at the very beginning; it sparked a fifteen-year-long debate online. People are always speaking on politics, religion, money, and everyone putting in their two cents on other people's personal lives. The list grows on and on. Everyone puts in their two cents, into a machine that does not accept any change or even dollar bills, but only accepts your time.

When I think about it, this is an adult world. The world slowly but surely is becoming a place that is no longer for children. The world is becoming a place that children are born in, just for reproductive legacies. It is so mandatory, our duty as adults to protect these children of the future. We need them; we need children to pass down our legacies and knowledge. However, I strongly do not believe that children should learn adult ways so prematurely. These children are watching things on television, in pop music, on social media, subjects that adults may not be so quickly adapted to themselves. What children are getting exposed to, by so much raw content from the adult world, it is making them fast forward through their childhoods. Whether it is pornography, drugs, smoking, drinking, and now vaping is a new addiction. It is so crucial for adults to groom and mold these young ones into productive citizens. I just fear that we are losing them, mentally. Childhood is so short-lived compared to adulthood; some adults tend to forget what it was like to be a child.

So, yea, the way I look at the world that adults have created, it is not a place for children anymore. Now obviously, I have to elaborate more on this statement, so here is what I mean by this. The world is not a safe place for children anymore. It is a place where children are born and have to be protected. This world is an adult world; controlled by adults. Children cannot have much of a say on the decisions made in this world. In the adult world, there is human trafficking, sex trafficking; there are kidnappings, child abuse, child molestation, child abandonment, and neglect.

What is also a severe issue for children is childhood obesity and school shootings. Children are so fragile in this adult world. Of course, it is a different perspective when it comes to parenting, and children are everything to their families. Children carry on the last name of their fathers, carrying on their legacies. But when it comes to running a corporation, politics, or country, children have to take the backseat on those positions. Children cannot vote, gamble, run for office; they have no real labor value to society. Children cannot be your doctor, prescribing your medication, or perform surgical procedures on you. Children cannot be airline pilots; flying you to your destination. Children cannot do much of anything besides being kids. In time, of course, as children become older, and become a mature adult, then they will get to have a say and have the rights of an adult. Yes, there are some child prodigies out there who have an essential voice. I just hope they know that the value of their voice is worth so much more than the likes and views they receive on their social media pages.

I also think about the kids who further their education by heading off to college and then graduating, earning their degrees. That is the feeling of being born again. Not as an infant child, but as a legal adult in the real world. Those kids, who are now legal adults, will then have to search for a job; they will go on those job interviews, expected by the employers, to come into that interview with "confidence." But it is tough for these kids to walk into these interviews with confidence, knowing they are in tens of thousands of dollars of debt, some even in debt in the six-figures. Instead of going to those job interviews with confidence, they go in with desperation. Willing to settle for a job that has nothing to do with their degrees. So, where do these kids find their "confidence" now? That is right, social media! They are seeking validation from their peers, while in return, their peers are seeking validation from them.

I pray that you; young people, do not get caught up in the dialogues of paranoid madness. You all have the power to stop and disconnect. Strengthen your bonds through reality. Let us no longer connect as people just through our struggles, our diseases, our victimization, and the negativity. Let us connect through our love for one another. Our non-perfect being selves. Connect with being alive and being focused. Let us wake up and finally unite. Unite in actual unity and not in division.

10 *Likes*

Anxiety, I Love to Hate You

I could not wait to get to this chapter. Anxiety is the one disorder I wish God did not instill in us to have. I am just going to say it simply, and I believe everyone who reads this can relate to me. Anxiety is the bane of my existence. Every single day, anxiety shows its joker like face. But the scariest thing about anxiety, is how it can transform its look from one person to thousands in a matter of seconds. Anxiety is the reason that I cannot go to a concert, like ever. If I was inside an arena, filled with tens of thousands of screaming fans. Surrounded by these random strangers, these faces I never seen before. Fireworks, explosions, all the excitement in the air. Then all of a sudden, I would feel it, anxiety coming for me like the predator is hunting me in its invisible stealth camouflage. It is so crazy because this is all in my head.

I would imagine myself being at a concert like that. I would picture myself inside, having a good seat, and then the show starts. Next thing I know, I am just looking around and observing all these different people. As I look around at all of these random people, and because of my anxiety, I would just think something so at random and bizarre like, "we are all going to die one day." I know that sounds hilariously crazy, but it is the truth. Like every last one of us, all ten or twenty thousand of us in that concert is going to be dead and buried one day. I do not know why; I know that sounds insane, but that is what comes to mind in those moments. My anxiety would just jack up; I would start breathing heavily, and I would completely ruin my night at that concert. But the ironic thing is, I could walk up and down the streets of Manhattan all day long, walk around Times Square, with hundreds of thousands of random people and be perfectly fine. So, I guess it just happens during different scenarios.

Anxiety is strange; I do not know what causes me to have such fear. I had to ask myself, "When was the first time I had an anxiety attack experience?" That is when it hit me, and I remembered when; it was at my uncle's funeral, my uncle Shane, who was my father's youngest brother. My uncle was a great man, a great human being. He always had a smile on his face when I would see him. Every time I would go spend time with him at his house, he would ask me, "*Hey Jordie, you want some olives man*?" He knew I loved olives or those pickle chips. Being that I was much younger back then, I did not realize that he had health issues, and would get sick often. My uncle Shane loved wearing these racecar jackets with all the sponsor patches attached to the coat, and the famous Superman t-shirt. In my eyes, he was Superman because he fought long and hard with his disease until he could no longer fight it anymore.

At his funeral, his mother, my grandmother, invited her pastor to come and speak at my uncle's funeral. As I was sitting there, next to my mother, I was listening to the pastor talk about death. The pastor said, "*It doesn't matter where you live, you can't hide from it; death will find you.*" That is when I realized that this thing called "death" is going to come to me someday. Not just me, but to all of us, to those we love, to those we once knew, to everyone. At that moment, I had my first anxiety attack, right there at my uncle Shane's funeral. I started breathing so hard; I lost focus. I just wanted to get up out of the chair and get the hell out of there. It messed me up; I was never the same after hearing that. It was how the pastor said it as well; his tone of voice made death seem like a punishment. Even though I did not like how the pastor said it, what he said was true. There is no hiding from death. Does not matter how rich or successful you are on this earth. Nothing can stop the process of getting old, being on your death bed, and then eventually moving forward to the next life.

I still struggle with that to this day. I still struggle with the thought of dying and how we, as Americans, we seem to have an infatuation with the dead. Some in a necrophiliac way and others through edibles, if you know what I mean. It is because of my dysfunctional relationship with death; I have a much more respectable consciousness with not just human life, but also animal life. Some people do not love a cow or a pig, but they love steaks and bacon cheeseburgers. People do not have a chicken as a pet, but people love a good two-piece, deep-fried. My point with all of this, why is it okay for people to accept eating other living beings? People eat the flesh of cows, chickens, pigs, turkeys, fish, and even ducks, yet when we lose our loved ones, we are never the same again? To be honest, I do not invest in the Holy Bible as much, but in the bible, I believe it says, "*Thou shall not kill.*" But it does not say, "*Thou shall not kill ONLY HUMANS*!" Think about this; none of these animals taste good at all without "plant-based seasoning," am I right? I genuinely believe now, when I did not eat live foods, such as fruits and vegetables, that nurtures us on a cellular level. When I only ate the flesh of another being; it tasted good, yes; but afterward, I could feel the pain that animal endured in the slaughterhouse.

I was ignorant when I ate animal products, and at the time, I did not care. I thought human life was the most superior and superficial. It is ironic because cows are much larger than us humans. When I realized how much weight I was putting on from all the animal intake, and how sick I was feeling after eating animal flesh. I realized that you are what you eat. When you eat the dead flesh of another being, you will become dead on the inside. At least that is how I felt after eating meat. I felt dead mentally, physically, and spiritually. Meat consumption did not help my anxiety. It most definitely refueled it; that is for sure.

I say all of that to say this; in our society, we love the dead. We worship dead people, we love dead animal flesh as food, and we love to give women dead flowers as a symbol of romance. Yes, I said dead flowers; those roses are ripped from its roots, so they really are freshly dead and only have a week to look good before they deteriorate. That is why I do not like giving women flowers. To me, it is bad luck. That is one of the reasons why I decided to go plant-based, and if I can help it, this will be a permeant life choice. I hear people say, "you have to eat meat; that is where you get your protein." Some may not know; animals, such as cows, live on a plant-based diet. So, the protein a cow internally possesses; is simply recycled protein from all the grass and the grains that a cow eats. So, in a way, cows are just a middleman for your daily source of protein, if you choose to eat meat.

But here is an epiphany for you. Since people receive their protein from a cow, where do you think people receive their stress, their mood swings, their depression, and guess what, their anxiety? Where do you think people get their anxiety? Exactly! The same animal flesh that people receive their source of recycled protein is the same animal flesh that has all of the recycled stress, recycled mood swings, recycled depression, and recycled anxiety these animals are enduring every single day. They are being tortured to death, just so we could love them as food on our breakfast, lunch, and dinner plates. Now I understand why people bless their food before they eat it. People pray that the food gives them nourishment, yet the meat and dairy give them illnesses, unfortunately. Forgive me for saying this, but I can no longer see dead animal flesh on a plate and call that a meal; I call that a funeral. But like I said, I cannot tell anyone how to live their lives, nor do I pass judgment on anyone. What I am saying is just food for thought; no pun intended.

But yes, I love to hate anxiety. I deal with it sporadically, but when it hits me, it hits me hard, at random, and blindsided. It is all in my head, that is what makes it so frustrating for me. Nothing could be wrong, and then I will just think about something that can go wrong, or death comes to mind for no apparent reason. Then all of a sudden, I would just stand up and think to myself, "Oh God! Oh God! Oh God! Oh God!" Then I would just tell myself in my mind, "Toughen up Jordan! Snap out of that and be tough!" That would usually calm me down and give me serenity. I do not know why that happens. Anxiety is this rush of unsolicited energy, racing to my brain, coming to crash the intellectual party.

My uncle's funeral was the first of many anxiety attacks. I do not wish anxiety on anyone. However, I think we all have our moments, whether we want them or not. Anxiety and fear prevent me from going to concerts, getting on rides at amusement parks; I cannot even drink caffeinated coffee. One cup of caffeinated coffee and my heart rate goes rapid, as if my heart is the DJ at a techno party. I avoid watching the news as best as I can. I feel that every time I turn on the news, there is murder, mass shootings, wildfires, new diseases, resurrected diseases, corrupted politics, police brutality, and so forth.

What I find so deeply disturbing is the newscast having to keep a straight face, with very little emotion while they address the tragedies of the world. I ask myself, is America a country, or is it just a corporation? Just a place of business, and not a place of humanity. When I took my anxiety and put that in the same bed with social media, that was one of the worst mistakes. Having four different news feeds to maintain, scrolling up and down, watching everyone else living a fabulous life, a life only I could imagine living at the time. My eyes, seduced with the temptation to post, to keep up with successful updates. I was posting hopeful dreams, posting "just wait until you see this," type of captions under my selfies. The adrenalin was running at full speed, dopamine free falling from my brain to the bottom of my feet. Then I feel the energy rising back up, like a volcanic eruption about to break out the top of my skull, and my whole body beginning to shake, like an earthquake.

I do not know, to this day, why I was shaking when I would see something on social media. I believe it is because, all these years of having a smartphone, I have heard my ringtones and notifications go off tens of thousands of times, along with my alarm clock. As I mentioned before, there were times when I would not even have my phone in my pocket. I would think I am feeling a vibration in my pocket as if my phone was inside my pocket. I would believe I hear the notifications of my phone sound off. But when I checked, nothing was there. These smartphones were scaring the hell out of me. I was indeed losing my mind over my social media and smartphone addiction. Now I understand when some people who have drug and alcohol addictions, those people say, "the drugs and the alcohol call for me." It calls for them to come for drinks, to get high, to destroy themselves. Social media was calling me; my phone was ringing in my mind. Even when I slept, I heard it.

That brought out the worst in me. This problem I had was the unnecessary anxiety I was feeling every single day. If I was in school while I was addicted, and there were smartphones like the phones of today, I would have failed out. There would have been no focus left within me whatsoever. The sad part about my addiction to social media was that I stopped using it purposefully towards my work, my acting career, or anything worthwhile. I only cared about the attention I was getting on those platforms and liking posts of beautiful women just to get their attention. I was scrolling up and down, searching for answers, so distracted that I would not even hear my name called. I was not living; this was programming at its worst, and I most certainly was programmed.

Until that one day when I could not take it anymore; that August 25th day. That was one of the worst days of my life. Anxiety had invaded my mind, my soul, and my body that terrible morning. I could not breathe properly; my legs were shaking; I just wanted to scream. I wanted so badly to call for help. But who can help you when you have a social media addiction? Who can help you with an addiction to social media, that is not considered a severe addiction, and how was I going to break free from this addiction and get rid of this anxiety?

Even though I love to hate anxiety, I must admit that anxiety keeps me somewhat humble. It keeps me human. I know that anxiety is going to be a part of my life until the very end. Anxiety is what lets me know; I do not have forever, but also that I do not need forever to be a better person or to have a great life. I do not need forever to be a better me, to live a better life. To live for today, to make a difference today, to help someone else's life, to change the world. All of those beautiful things can start today. Tomorrow may not be what is promised for us, but we can always make a change for a better today. So, in a way, I learned something from my experience with anxiety. I learned that even though I do not have forever on this earth, I learned to be okay with that. I am just grateful and blessed that I was chosen by my creator to experience this stage we call life; on this earth. I do not believe that the goal of life is to live forever because we cannot live forever. As I said before, time is a disease that we want to have forever, but death is an unstoppable cure.

I believe that one of our purposes on this earth is to defeat our egos and to know our true selves simply. Genuinely knowing ourselves and not trying to find ourselves through a job. Nothing in this world that can hire you or fire you can define you. Even though we as human beings can talk, we should never let words define us. That is why I always find the question, "Can you tell me about yourself?"

to be such an awkward question. How did we allow words and numbers to define us as human beings? When I was a kid, it hit me one day. I remember asking why do we as people have to pay taxes and use money? Of course, adults laughed at me and thought I was crazy. But as an adult, that little kid inside of me still asks that same question; why? You realize, us human beings; we are, have always been, and will always be, the only living species on this planet, that has to worry about money.

This is the truth; we as people are the only living species that have to worry about paying taxes, buying, selling, compensation, racism, rich and poverty, debt, bankruptcy, and then we die. We are the only living beings on earth that live through all of that chaos. No other mammals or animals have to be defined by these lifestyles. Every other species is free. Free to live the life they were born to live. Every other living being on this earth has the freedom to exist as they please. Every other living species on this planet does not look for answers, or ask to borrow money, or has a religion. Of course, I know this may all sound insane to some people. But if you think about it, the world has gone mad. Us humans are the ones who shoot birds from the sky, deer hunting, duck hunting, and even killing elephants for their ivory tusk.

We kill cows, chickens, pigs, and turkeys for restaurants and Thanksgiving dinners. We kidnap orca whales just for them to do some flips and tricks to entertain us. Do you want to know why you cannot sleep at night? Based on the knowledge of human anatomy, I now believe the human body was never designed to consume the flesh of other living things. We are herbivores. The human body is also highly intelligent. In theory, I believe the human body is smart enough to know the meat you are eating is not naturally meant for you to eat. Therefore, it identifies the animal flesh that you are eating, had to of been brutally slaughtered. Your body knows that the flesh of the animal you are eating suffered a horrific death.

The human body knows, one way or another, and by you seasoning the animal flesh to make it taste good, that does nothing but insult your body's intelligence. That is just you sugarcoating the dead tissue of another life. Being that our body is so intelligent, it then makes you feel the pain the animal felt when it was tormented. That energy; the pain and suffering those animals had to endure, is still within the flesh that you eat. So, when you have trouble sleeping at night, and your doctors call it "sleep apnea," I would prefer to call it guilt. The guilt that your body feels when it knows it is digesting foods you are not naturally or morally supposed to eat. You having trouble breathing while you sleep at night, is simply the same feelings of the animal having difficulty breathing while it was being crucified. As I said, I am a firm believer, more than ever now, that you are what you eat.

With all that said, once again, I cannot tell you what to do, what to eat, or how to live; it is your life. I make sure that I make myself clear about that; throughout this book. Just ask yourself a question; in fact, question everything. The way this world is being misinformed by social media; it is damn near impossible to seek the truth. Trying to find the truth on social media is like trying to find a teardrop in the ocean.

We have caused more harm and destruction on this planet then we believe. We cannot blame God or even Satan.

Blame ourselves; we have screwed this planet up for far too long. We have all done wrong, but if we can all do wrong, we can all do right, and we have to do right and fix these global issues before we go insane and give up on our civilization. Our actions, what we do, how we behave, is what defines who we are. If the actions of the masses do not change, if we continue to live on a western diet and put a blind eye to it, if we continue to dedicate our lives, our precious time to social media and smartphones, we will… Well, I guess I cannot say. Perhaps I do not know. We will see about that someday, right?

I deal with my anxiety to the best of my ability. When I removed myself from social media, my anxiety plummeted. One less thing, however, reality does still hit me in the face, and every so often, anxiety shows its disturbing presence. It is all in our minds; anxiety, I mean. I had to accept the fact that I am not in control of everything that happens in life, which is what gives me mixed feelings about death; the fear and anxiety that comes with death.

But when I think about little kids around the world, all the infants, who die every single day. I think about them and just say to myself, "how dare you?" There are children and babies in this world who do not live to reach a certain age. Babies who never had a chance to take their first step, children who did not make it to their junior or senior prom in high school. I took my first steps; I went to my prom. Yet I am afraid of death? Again, I say to myself, "how dare you?" It is so selfish to be fearful of death, knowing that many people in this world did not have the opportunity to reach the age that I have been blessed to reach. Anxiety is one thing, but life is way too damn short to be afraid of living it because of the fear of death. I refuse to spend my entire life, fearful of something that is destined to happen eventually. Then when it happens, I would spend the rest of eternity looking back at life, saying, "I should have done this, I wish I had done that." My greatest fear now is eternal regrets.

Let me say this as well; work is not your brother. Work is not your father, your mother, sister, not even your best friend. Even if you love your job, your job cannot love you in return; only the people at your job can love you back. So, if there is ever a moment in time when you need to connect with your friends or family, do that. Make it happen; do not let work or your egos get in the way of the bonds you have made with the people in your lives. What did I say before? Nothing that can hire you or fire you can define you. Reach out to those friends, reach out to those family members, and eat up those grudges. You never know if or when a tragedy is about to happen, leaving you with those regrets that will eat you alive. Money is for your wallet, but family and friends are for your heart. You already know what is most important; always follow your heart.

I completely understand and accept the fact that I cannot escape death. None of us can. But I can most definitely escape social media, and that is exactly what I did. I escaped, and if I can help it, I will not ever log back on. God willing; if I were to live to be a hundred and twenty-five years old, I still would not use these platforms or the new platforms to come, that may be more addictive then the platforms we have today. They are not worth it to me. We must remain human beings. We must recommit to the natural things we use to do. The natural things such as; going for a brisk walk; without a video post of you going for a brisk walk. Going to the beach without you taking a hundred pictures from multiple angles.

We have this thing in our minds called "memories." It is time we start to use them again and just be in the moment.

There is one thing we can never capture on video, and that is our dreams. Not our dreams as far as life goals, but the dreams of our sleep. So many dreams; so many perceptions I saw in my dreams. We cannot take pictures in our dreams; we cannot record videos, no screenshots, no likes, no views, or followers. To be in the moment of the dream. The dreams only last but so long, so we have to make the most of it. That sounds so much how life once was; before smartphones and social media, right? Life is a dream; that lasts only but a swift minute. I believe that we have lost that enthusiasm of life, the act of being in the moment, and enjoying the experience. Yes, we are lucky to have cameras for photos of family, friends, and loved ones. But I feel we have overwhelmed ourselves to the point of no return. We take pictures of our faces hundreds of times, taking fifteen to twenty minutes, just to edit and make one post. Then spend the rest of our day looking at the likes and comments we get from that one post. I have been there before. Life is truly meant to be lived, experienced, much more than it is to be photographed and posted about for numbers. It is crucial that we see each other as human beings again and not just these numbers of likes, views, and followers.

I am not perfect; we all have our flaws. Accidents happen; things go wrong that we cannot predict or explain why they occur. But we cannot go our whole lives being afraid. If there is anything you want out there in the world, find out what that is, and just start. Just understand; you will have three best friends that motivate you to achieve whatever it is that you want. Those friends are rejection, patience, and tomorrow. Those are the three friends that will be there with you every step of the way. You will hear many "no's," many rejections. But all it takes is that one "yes." The "big yes;" that can change your life. You know what? Do not wait for a yes or no from anyone. Do your own thing, make your way in life, and never delay your blessings by waiting for a random stranger to tell you yes. Take more control of your own life. People are going to do what they want regardless of what you tell them. Yes, it is okay that we care for others, and that we should always be kind to one another. But taking care of others is irrelevant if you are not taking care of yourself. So many people are social media influencers. Keep in mind; those influencers are still human. They have to go through life just like everyone else.

They may not have all the answers you are looking for; you may have answers for them at times. They go through depression and anxiety, just like me, just like you. I remember John Lennon's song "*Give Peace A Chance*." What I have learned about peace is that there is already peace on this earth. Peace has been on this earth for billions of years. God has created this peaceful world for all humanity to live in harmony. Harmony with animals and unity with ourselves. We, as humans, have lost sight of the peace on earth thousands of years ago. We do not know how to be at peace with each other. All we know how to be now; is be at war with ourselves—nuclear bombs, guns, bullets, assassinations, racism, terrorism, and hatred. We did not lose peace; peace has always been here. We have lost the perception of peace. It reminds me of this quote from William Blake, in his book "*The Marriage of Heaven and Hell*," "*If the doors of perception were cleansed, everything would appear to man as it is, infinite.*" This quote is actually how Jim Morrison came up with his rock band's name, "The Doors." The perception of how we live in this world is covered by a thick, deep fog of confusion and consumption. We could not see peace even if we were looking for it.

I do not know if we will ever see peace again in this lifetime. Too much blood has been shed. But that is what we hope for, isn't it? We hope that one day we can all see peace. Every time you see a sunrise, a sunset. Every time you go to the beach on a sunny day. Every time you sit on your porch on a rainy day and listen to the sound of rainfall. When you travel and see the mountains, the scenery, the world, you will see peace. But on social media, you will not see peace. You will see the darkness that we try so desperately to shy ourselves away from in the real world.

You see the worst in people, the absolute worst. You see the behaviors of people, and you say to yourself, "who raised them?" People are going crazy all over the world on their profiles, being seduced and controlled by those meaningless numbers. Seeing mass shooters go on live and shooting up a Jewish synagogue. This problem is a global social problem. We are at war, at war with ourselves. We could not see peace from World War I, from 1914 to 1918. We definitely could not see peace during World War II, from 1939 to 1945, and now I believe that we are peace blinded; more than ever before. The third World War is among us now; except this time, in this era, this war will be fought on a virtual battlefield. This war will be confronted with the most powerful tool the world has ever seen; "social media."

11 *Likes*

World War III: Social Media

This world war is the war that none of us saw coming—a war that affects everyone who has an account, everyone. There are over approximately two billion FB users. That is two-fourths of the world's population. Think about what kind of power you can have with the attention of two billion people. With just the right personality, with just the right amount of money, you can influence people to do just about anything that you want them to do. All four platforms: Franklin Benjamin, Ivory, Twitchell, and Sam Chapman, are free services. These free services, plus our free will, will then create free publicity, free chaos, free destruction, and free wars.

Look at how ugly people treat each other in today's world. I do not see presidential debates as debates anymore. I see enemies running for the presidency, shutting each other down. No one is listening or hearing anyone. People are getting cut off at mid-sentence, people saying, "I disagree with this, I disagree with that," or "you are not qualified to speak on certain topics." "You don't know what you are talking about." So many people are trying to be better than the next person. New friendships and relationships become short-lived because of differences of opinions on religions, sexuality, ethnicities, or nationalities. One group of people believing they are better than other groups. These are the social dynamics we are using to fight amongst each other, every single day. We attack each other's minds with disturbing comments and judgments. Some people will then take that same attitude and energy they showed on social media, and project it out into the real world, onto real people. We seriously are at war with ourselves every day.

Seeing the young ones in the world today; who cannot focus on what is important. They cannot focus on their education, their mental and physical health, their destiny, or their lives. They smile at a screen but frown at people's faces. People are bumping into things or other people as they walk, almost getting hit by cars because their headphones are too loud, or they are looking down, glued to their phones. Do we care anymore about anything out there in the real world? Will we even know how to care in the future? There is no telling what impact social media will have on the children of the next generation. Children who will believe that life is not life at all, without social media. To me, that is a psychological genocide to their minds worldwide.

These platforms are intoxicating their minds, preventing them from having the ability to think for themselves, being creative, to listen, and to love unconditionally. Have you noticed that we do not see anyone's eyes anymore? All we see are eyelids in the world. People's eyes are submissively focused on those screens, looking down. I tested it myself; as I write this in a classroom, I just looked at some young people. Heads are down, necks bent, looking at their phones, and I see nothing but eyelids. I wonder what they see. Do they see their future? Their dreams, perhaps? Maybe they see a whole bunch of chaos that tells them what to do, what to think, and what to feel, particularly about themselves.

My God; if these machines were to stop. This world would possibly come to a devastating end. I do not believe these kids could even survive seven whole days without social media or having their smartphones; adults either. Imagine all of social media crashing, never to return. There are people out there who would die. Suicides, purge like murders, emotional explosions, totally disconnected from reality. A reality that we fear would come into existence one day. Who would have thought that technology could one day be the cause of our doomsday? I am not saying this is going to happen; I am not trying to predict this to happen. But the way we are going with all of the world's social issues, trying to solve global problems, through apps. There indeed will be no future for the youth. I see a lot of machines doing the work, which will dismiss our productivity. That will then slow us down, break us down, and then kill us all by being worthless to our society, and also to ourselves. Social media has transformed into new nuclear weapons. The new weapons of mass destruction, where you do not even have to leave your seat to be attacked. Nations upon nations attacking each other with derogatory comments. All of the information and data you post; photos from your private lives being exposed at random. Leaked information and false news at its worst, confusing the minds of not millions, but billions of people every day; every hour, minute, and second.

There is a saying, "the mind is a terrible thing to waste." I say, "the mind is a terrible thing to confuse." Politics in America have created so much confusion, to the point where I see it as a distraction. So many lies in so many eyes. I will be honest; I do not know much about politics, as of right now. But I am learning little by little, educating myself as best as I can. Politics has become very frustrating and unmotivating to follow. I believe that since social media emerged, people with their platforms have been able to form an enormous following based on their political views. People do not have to even run for office; just have a large following on social media. If you receive enough likes and retweets, you are then considered a famous political expert. That is another thing about politics; popularity is politicians' newest addiction.

Being highly popular in America is like being a God. Famous people can motivate and even manipulate the masses so easily. However, what I find so disturbing with politics, is how people are just treating themselves so piss poorly; so inhumanly. Many politicians with fragile egos, going head to head with each other, which then leaks down to the general public to have open discussions, or even their debates online. That is when the real war begins, not just with the citizens of America's society, but societies all over the world.

Electing a president has changed forever. After researching what happened with the election of 2016, Cambridge Analytica using FB to manipulate the public. The company used the data of millions of FB users to create ads for Donald Trump's campaign, which led Trump to achieve an arranged victory over Hilary Clinton. Russia allegedly assisted that. Quite the chess moves to make, huh? I guess you can say that social media has contributed to politicians' campaigns since 2008, with the presidential run of Barack Obama and John McCain. It is so intriguing how people's minds change so quickly now, as far as who they will support. All it takes is one Ad, one post, one meme, and you would lose thousands of votes in seconds; just by changing the minds and behaviors of the general public. Social media has changed the political game forever.

Now, Trump is the most hated man in America; from the blue side, but the red team, they cannot get enough of him. Every time you turn on the news, every newspaper, online articles, social media, you cannot go a day without seeing his name or face. Here is my take on this human being; Donald Trump. Yes, I did call him a human being; even though his act is not right, he is still only human. My take is I do not hate this man, nor do I love this man. I do not even know this man to love or hate him. I never met him before, never sat down and had a conversation with him; and at this point, I definitely would not want to. I do hate what he has undone in this country—making this country more chaotic than ever. I hate what he has done to the minds of the American people, basically re-activating the racist tendencies in our society. Trump turned the United States of America into the Divided States of America. What I hate the most is he uses Twitchell as his diary. Except it is not so secret or private, Trump wants the world to see exactly how he thinks and feels at all times.

I believe that Trump's presidential run was a personal choice; that had nothing to do with America, but it had everything to do with himself. Trump himself even said in an interview back in the eighties that he would never run for president. Why the change of heart? Was it because he strongly did not approve of the Obama administration? Simply because Obama's skin tone did not qualify Obama of being a respectable president with high intelligence? Was it because Trump was bored with his life; and needed something much more productive to do besides his television show "The Apprentice?" Perhaps he ran for president simply because he was; afraid. I believe that to understand people, good or bad, even the kind of people with a method to their madness; you have to put yourself in their shoes.

I Look at this man Donald Trump, who is now a seventy-three-year-old senior citizen. He has been a boss for decades, who never had to answer to anyone. He has been through the love and marriage phase several times, had his children, and now grandchildren. He has traveled the world several times already; met all the celebrities he could. All the success, power, and money; what more can Trump look forward to in his life, other than his death? Remember what I said earlier; it does not matter how wealthy you become, from the poorest to the most prosperous; we all must face our death. I do not know what Trump's take on death is, but I am sure, like any other human being, there is some type of fear within. Some kind of anxiety that comes with it; just how I described the anxiety I felt at my uncle's funeral.

All the billions; all the money in the world cannot stop the process of aging and getting older. I bet Trump woke up early one morning, splashed some water on his face, looked in the mirror, and said, "For the love of God, I'm getting old." Trump is no longer that "handsome" looking man in his thirties or forties; that some women would have loved to have been with; men who would have loved to work for him, or even become him. Trump is older now; his face has changed, the world has changed, and there was a moment in life that he realized that he was not on top of the world anymore.

So, what does Trump do at that point? Trump goes against his word some thirty years later and runs for president. Then Trump wins the election. The Republicans gave him that power back. They gave him that taste of being important again and being the talk of the town. People gave him instant validation through votes, likes, and retweets. I think more in-depth into this whole Trump slogan, "Make America Great Again," I see something different. I do not believe any of Trump's presidency was for the benefit of the American people or America. If you read beneath the slogan, what it says is "Make Trump Great Again," or even "Make Me Great Again." After all, the word "me" is in the name "America."

But again, I do not know this man. Is what I just said about Trump completely accurate? Probably not on a personal level. But from human to human, I believe so. I think Trump is just an older man, living with a social media addiction, living life with fear and paranoia. Some may say Trump is fearless, but no courageous president is going to build a wall, to keep other people out. The way this whole system is in America, with Trump's administration; this was a flying plane with no landing gear, destined to crash. I would just say that when it comes to Trump; the moral of the story is; you cannot clean something, with dirt on your hands. What I mean by that is Trump, not being an experienced politician, had no idea what he was getting himself into, diving headfirst in the pool of presidency. You have to be almost squeaky clean, no criminal records, no accusations, just basically being a respectable, taxpaying American citizen. Those qualifications probably did not sit well for Trump. You cannot run a country being wet behind the ears, having done a lot of corruption and attacking that Trump has done since day one. I learned that a businessman and being a politician are not the same, but the experience of the two just rhymes. Social media was a powerful weapon used to help Trump be elected. We shall see what the future holds with this man and the future of America.

I have this other theory about America and the American flag. I thought this some time ago. I think of the old American flag, with the thirteen stars representing the first thirteen states formed by the British colonies. Then I see the current American flag with all fifty stars. I see the colors; red, white, and blue. When I look at the blue square with the fifty stars on the flag, I begin to think about the hidden purpose, a hidden agenda. The blue square went from thirteen stars to fifty stars, right? So, my theory is, the blue square is a blueprint of America.

I believe America is still trying to expand its territory globally. Now I understand why every time that America fights in a war, America keeps a base camp in that country. I wondered why Alaska and Hawaii, which are farther away from the other states, are part of the United States. I believe America's ultimate goal is to take over land all over the world. I would not be surprised if a few more stars are included on the American flag, sometime in the future. The American flag is meant to grow, meant to add more stars, but other countries are saying, "No! Not without a fight, you will." Is this why America has been at war since before there even was the United States of America? Is this why America will always be at war in our lifetime? One nation, under God, right? America has unfinished business; it is still growing as a country, or should I say corporation.

We, as a nation, have opened up the doors of opportunity for the worst people, this past presidential election. Politicians that are just unrelatable, wearing the same suits, same faces, agendas of corruption, chaos, and greed. After witnessing the last three years of politics, I hope an entertainer is never elected president in this country ever again. Even if the entertainer is a creative genius, I do not believe politics were designed for creative geniuses or entertainers. A creative genius and entertainer can discuss politics and be politically conscious, of course. However, a creative genius may have a hard time following rules, and there are most definitely rules enforced in the highest position in America. To run a country, govern a state, be a mayor of a city; that calls for some political experience; even though Trump has remedied that outcome. The difference with Ronald Reagan is the fact that Reagan was Governor of California from 1967 to 1975 and served his country during World War II. There was at least some patriotic action on Regan's resume.

However, Regan's era was the crack cocaine era, along with the HIV and AIDS epidemic. It was not the best time in history for the American people, especially the African American and Latino communities. But that part of American history is for another book. I am sure not many have ever acknowledged this, but when you think about it, Donald and Ronald? What did I say earlier? A businessman and a politician are not the same; they just rhyme.

But as I said before, I do not hate Trump; I do not love Trump. When it comes down to people; If you do not love or hate them, you commit no wasted energy to them. I am just really appalled at the skullduggery of actions and behavior Trump has performed these past several years in office. After my experiences of voting these past twelve years, I do not feel that I can ever support or participate in either party, Democratic or Republican. I will have to go independent. Neither political party, I think, has been of great benefit to all American people, especially the African American, Latino, and the native American people? Forget about it. The natives of this land were given no respect since the beginning. With all the wars, all the battles, all the debates, minorities are still being tragically and brutally murdered, with no care in the world. I am not saying that I will never vote again. I am saying that both political parties are only playing the same game that started in the year 1828 for Democrats and 1854 for Republicans. The same game has been played, with the same rules of keeping the masses of the minorities inferior, and the white's superior. I refuse to participate in either party; I am going purple. I may have to vote blue one more time for this upcoming election. That is all I have to say about that.

I do not believe that Republicans who voted for Trump are evil people. Many people are just being loyal and bias to the Republican party. People have every right to vote for who they want to vote for; as do I. We cannot help ourselves, getting caught up in the hype; I certainly did with Barack Obama. I got caught up in the hype; seeing the first African American president ahead in office was a pipe dream. I still find it unbelievable that Obama won; twice. When I look at the timeline of all the United States presidents, and I see forty-three white men and one African American. Even though Obama is half African and half white, I will take it! We were halfway there as the black culture. I found that timeline to be very much so; a symbol of change; that was well overdue. From 1776 to 2006-7, nothing but white men were running this country. Then Obama came into office. I am sure many black people were expecting this man to change the black communities. But now I understand that it does not work like that. If you want to make changes in anything, you have to start with the politics within the community first. People have to vote for the right mayors, then voting for the right governors, then making your way up the political ladder. I knew Obama was only going to be able to do but so much; for the African American communities across the country. I guess you can say I was naïve when I voted for him.

It was the first time I voted, turning eighteen years old. I just wanted to support the impossible, that became possible. When I look back at Obama's presidential run, that sparked up the racial wars in America again.

You would have thought O.J. Simpson won the election the way people hated Obama. Black friends were losing white friends and vice versa. Causing Trump to go against his word and run in the 2016 race, just to undo everything Obama has done. Could you imagine if Trump ran against Obama? Boy, would that have been a showdown to remember!

The presidential race of the century! One last thing about Obama; there perhaps are many black people out there who are still angry with Obama, feeling that he did nothing for his people. Well, I think it is best to show a little forgiveness. Obama went into the White House, with a head full of black hair. By the time he came out of office, his hair was damn near all white. God knows the kind of stress, anxiety, chaos, and issues that man had to endure, while in office. The issues of America colonized his hair and turned it completely white. I cannot fully blame this man. You cannot go into a system that was historically designed to protect and prioritize one specific group of people, and expect to change that overnight, or even in eight years. He may not have done all that he could for his people. But a black man becoming president of the United States of America, for the very first time; for black people, that is equivalent to having the first man on the moon. How would you expect this man to work miracles in a racist society?

His eight years as president, for me, was eight years of inspiration. A symbol of black potential, but an unfortunate absence of remembrance. I do not remember much of his role as president. I cannot recall much of a monumental moment during the two terms, except the capturing and killing of Osama Bin Laden. I just saw this "too cool for school" kind of guy that made history, but I do not know much about his story. I feel that black people were as anticipated for Obama to win the election as they were for O.J. Simpson being acquitted during "the trial of the century."

I do not know where this country is heading in the future, let alone this entire world. Oceans are becoming more polluted by the minute. The health of people is starting to decline horrifically; health care cost is now in the neighborhood of the trillions. They do not see a break from this health crisis. But what do we have to keep us distracted? That wonderfully hypnotic social media. A few use social media to spread awareness. Yet, some people rather see drama, negativity, and provoking fear in the minds of millions. People are pointing fingers, blaming Muslims, calling them terrorists, Christians, Jews, and atheists. People blaming politics, creating doubt in many if there even is a God looking down on us. Social media has the power to convince the public not to worry, not to panic, just stay entertained. Convincing the public that these "likes," and retweets will change the world; when all they do is fuel the egos and keep people hiding behind applications. People are just so ugly with each other, pretending that it is just a friendly conversation; that it is all love. There is no such thing as virtual love. They are symbols of love but do not believe in the hype that social media has created.

A change must happen indefinitely. Having billions of people bring their social issues to these social media platforms. Chaotic culture wars are bound to happen—the constant attacks of each other online. People using words as their weapons to attack others from different ethnic groups, and the hashtags spread the dark messages; God, help us all! Social media has become a psychological battlefield; looking to destroy your hope, produce more fear, stress, and anger.

The movements that are created on social media are virtual armies with large followings. Cult followings even; People getting you to do whatever they want you to do. They can manipulate you, lie to you, and also take money from you. As I said, can you imagine social media being around during the years of Hitler? Hitler; having all of that power and influence in a smartphone, right there in the palm of his hand.

You know, looking at the timeline of all the U.S. presidents, when Obama won, I felt that America passed the finish line, and finally achieved its truest potential in our society. But once again, I was wrong. We went backwards, way back. Do you know what is really sad about today's world being in this social media climate? History repeated itself, and now we have the smartphones to record it all. They are documenting the same decisions, the same mistakes, and the same racist system that has been in effect since day one of America. That is the next thing I want to talk about in the following chapter. The one method that has yet cease to exist. Racism!

12 *Likes*

Racism on Social Media

When I was a kid in my seventh grade English class, I remember doing these summaries for a couple of short stories I read through in my English book. I do not remember the name of the short stories. Still, I remember my English teacher being frustrated with me about misunderstanding the message of the stories. My English teacher screamed out that one of the stories is about racism. I was eleven years old back then. At that age, I knew nothing about racism. Up to that particular point in my life, I only saw the violence among African Americans in the city I grew up in as a kid. I only knew how to defend myself among other African Americans because we were the only ones living in that environment. The only time I saw white people around the area was in school, as my teachers or in the community as law enforcement officers.

For the life of me, I did not understand the violence between black people. I did not know why we were so hostile towards each other, so judgmental and hateful among our peers. Where did all of this anger amongst us come from every day? I did not understand this at eleven years old. Perhaps me being quiet and shy for so many years had taken its toll on me, even held me back from teaching myself certain things. Maybe I should have read more books, not just to have the information, but to understand why these situations occur in society. Growing up in the environment that I did, not understanding the violence, not wanting to participate in it, it made me not want to accept being black fully. I used to see myself as mixed with black and some white because I was much lighter in my complexion than my family was. I know that sounds very ignorant and trivial; that is because it is. But again, I was just a kid.

To see all the fighting, cursing, and gang activity, the drinking and drugging. I thought that was what being black was all about, and I was not that type of person; I was not that kid. Growing up, I did not see much inspiration. I knew if I wanted to get out of there, out of the hood, I was on my own. I realized that I had to get busy and buckle down on my schoolwork so that I could one day leave. Racism was still something I did not experience because I did not leave the area, except when I went on vacation. I only saw the violence we had in the black community; however, I was beginning to acknowledge the racism in America and the world. I just had to find a way to deal with the violence in my community.

Now let me be clear; it was not horrible all the time; for the most part, I kept to myself and stayed focused with school, football, and wrestling after school; and then went home. My life growing up in East Orange, New Jersey, was not entirely a bad experience for me; it was pretty decent. There was not much inspiration, but I made the best of it, for the first seventeen years of my life. I had to be an inspiration to myself. Although my high school football coaches kept me in check, along with some of my teachers, they have children of their own to tend to, so I knew I had to figure some things out for myself.

It was not until I went off to college, into the somewhat semi-real world, that I got a whiff of racism. Going off to college was a completely different experience; I was now, from a visual standpoint, a minority in the environment. Centenary College is where my eyes and mind opened up to our society and how the relationship between black and white correlated. From my college experience, I met some beautiful people; white, black, Asian, middle eastern, from all different parts of the world, and mixed walks of life. I also met some people who were quite the opposite of beautiful. There were some individual experiences where I had to deal with racism and prejudice people in that environment. Not on campus, but in the area, I came across a few ignorant people. There were some people that I thought would be a friend of mines for a long time, but then after college was a wrap, so was that "friendship." A lot of unfollows on social media, and people who blocked me. People I had to let go of because there were some very racial derogatory comments said on FB, from people that I knew, or at least I thought I knew. I learned a few disappointing things about people on those platforms. People will tolerate you if they have to work with you, but once that is no longer the case, you will know who "a friend of yours," is. The real world begins to welcome you in. I guess that is just part of the American ritual for black people, not only in America but all over the world.

Many of my experiences of racism and prejudice were from a customer to employee basis. I encountered many racist people in those scenarios. I could just feel the tension, the negative energy coming off of them. Even though I try my best not to assume that is the case. Some of those employees I dealt with probably had a bad day of work, hated their job, or had some personal issues that they were going through. However, I came across some racist, disrespectful employees who were ignorant and just unhappy people. I was no longer that naïve eleven-year-old kid that did not understand racism. Not only do I know it for what it is, but I also experienced it.

Now, racism has found another way, another platform to emerge its diseased energy. Racism has found social media. Seeing young white college kids putting on blackface for Halloween and then posting pictures on social media as if there is nothing wrong or racists about that. America is not even the only place in the world that performs this racist act; this is an actual tradition all across the globe. Blackface has taken place in countries such as; Netherlands, Spain, Iran, Germany, Austria, Japan, Mexico, South Africa, and other locations across America. Social media is showing you all the ignorance that takes place all over the world. It is as if racism is a popular way of life for some people. But the sad thing is that every single non-black culture is fascinated with the black culture. From our music, our fashion statement, even our swag. But when an innocent unarmed black person falls victim to police, a racist, or even by another black person, those same people are nowhere to be found, culturally neglectful.

As long as the black culture is profitable, our presence will be tolerated. I find that to be disgusting and shameful. People love black celebrities, black athletes who make millions, billions for their leagues, who have millions of followers on social media. Yet, there is so much backlash when black athletes take a stand. When I think about "Exiled" NFL player Colin Kaepernick, yes, I said Exiled-NFL player and not ex-NFL player because he was exiled out of the league for taking a political stand. He sacrificed his career, a multi-million-dollar career, by taking a knee during the national anthem. He took a stand against police brutality, the social injustices, and the racism of society. That was one of the most monumental moments not in just sports history, but American history. Something I would never have thought to do. A black man who exercised his first amendment right. To some, he is a hero; but to others, he is disrespecting the flag, the country, and all of the men and women who fought and died for America.

When Kaepernick was blacklisted for his actions, it compelled so many posts, many comments, so many tweets, even Trump had to weigh in on the subject and call Kaepernick a "son of a bitch." Black and white people at war yet again. One thing I must say to people, and I will keep this simple. "Do not say or do the wrong things, just because you have the right to do them." Colin Kaepernick did what he believed in his heart was right, regardless of the consequences that came his way. But to have people be so ignorant, blinded by their bias thoughts; it just showed me, indefinite, that racism is a way of life, possibly for life, for some people. Racism just may be here to stay, and people are going to fight to the death to keep this economical, white superiority behavior alive and, most importantly, relevant. That number seven jersey became a symbol that will go down in history. A symbol that says, "break the toxic traditions that were designed to break you."

Even though social media is not necessarily reality, some people who post racist tweets have not come to the fact that everyone is still watching them. When you see people posting a comment using the n-word or other derogatory phrases; they do not realize that law enforcement is watching them; their co-workers, black co-workers, their supervisors, and their bosses. Chances are people will be held accountable for their online actions. Even a few non-black celebrities who use the n-word on social media, as if no one can see it, then afterward have to tweet out an apology. It is difficult to tell who the adults are and who the children are behind these social media platforms. When I was online, I could not tell at all. But let me tell you; if you ever want to lose your job, just send out a few racists tweets. Twitchell is in the business of helping you get a pink slip.

Apologies on social media are so insincere. They are just easily posted, and people believe that others will accept their apologies with "likes." Like the whole Botham Jean and Amber Guyger's situation. I do not believe one bit of that story that was told about what happened that night. I will not go into details about what I think happened; I was not there. However, the story that Guyger told about mistaking Jean's apartment with her own; and then being so scared that she shot him twice, in his own home. The day I believe that will be the day doctors say eating pork is extremely good for your heart. But that is not why I brought this whole Jean and Guyger situation up. I brought it up because of the power of a racist's tears, the power of a racist's apologies, and the way the family of Botham Jean, the bailiff, and the judge forgave this woman for her sins. They forgave and comforted Guyger before she even did five seconds of her prison sentence. That took my breath away. How could one forgive so quickly? As far as Botham Jean's younger brother, who is still a teenager, with a child's heart. A child's heart that is filled with forgiveness, and not to mention; who is a Christian. A child who was very much in pain from the loss of his brother, who may not be thinking clearly, and who was also in a very vulnerable state of mind. Perhaps Jean's brother, Brandt Jean, just wanted to feel his brother, through Guyger, and feel his brother's last moments of life through her, which is why he hugged her.

Forgive me, but I cannot microwave forgiveness. Forgiveness does not come that quickly for me, in my heart. If someone who I believed to be a racist, is responsible for taking the life of one of my family members, forgiveness would not be opened for discussion. It is out of the question. I do not believe I can ever forgive someone for taking one of my family member's life. It is one thing when car accidents occur, but when it comes to guns and bullets, I honestly do not believe it is anyone's time to go, in that particular circumstance.

I do not believe that God has anything to do with people losing their lives from gun violence. Guns are a human-made weapon. Our society, American society, has to take some drastic action to make our country a safer, healthier, and productive environment for the children of today and those to come in the future.

I always wondered; why is racism still so current to today's world? Why is that so? So, I thought about it, got very in-depth, and I believe that I found a theory; two theories on why racism is still current. I think in general, not as individuals, just in general, white people in America, since the birth of this nation, to this day, does not need black people for employment. When was the last time you heard of a white person chasing down a black person for a job? You just do not see that on a general note in the real world. It always seems that black people are the ones who are still searching for jobs, and white people are the ones who hire us. It has been this way since the very beginning. My second theory is this; again, generally speaking, not individually; white people do not need black people to love them. You may have great individual relationships with people of other ethnicities. Still, in general, white people do not need love from the African American or Latino communities.

Companies owned by white people may appreciate us as consumers. However, buying someone's product is not love; it may be just a love for the products. That is why when you see things online such as H&M, having a young African American child modeling a hoodie that reads, "The Coolest Monkey in The Jungle." Because of our history in America, with African Americans referred to as monkeys, this incident caused outrage. Another example was Gucci coming out with a women's black turtleneck sweater, long enough for the turtleneck to cover half of the woman's face, with a hole that shows the woman's lips. Around that hole, there is a red oval shape that resembles lips, and if you do some research, the sweater looks precisely like "blackface." I brought those examples up to support my theories on why racism is still in existence in our society. Because the general public of white people does not need black people for employment or love, they can get away with disrespect, with stereotypes and stigmas and even murder.

I just thank God that social media was not around during the first half of the twentieth century, with the unapologetic mind state of racism back then. One would imagine; the n-word being said all around social media, the n-word as a hashtag, or even live recordings of a lynching. We would have seen hell on earth for sure. Possibly could have seen segregated social media platforms. How I see it, as long as the general white population does not need the general black population for making a living or for love, the system of racism will continue to be practiced for hundreds of years to come.

I had an epiphany about racism and how it correlates with gangs in America; the Bloods, the Crips, and the Ku Klux Klan. Have you ever realized, three of the most notorious gang organizations in American history, are symbolically represented by the same colors of the American flag? Red for the Bloods, white for the Klan, and blue for the Crips? That cannot be a coincidence. That was strategically orchestrated that way; to keep the decreasing of African Americans progressing. It was like the white started on the east coast, and brutally made their way to the west coast. Then red and blue started on the west coast and ruthlessly made their way over to the east coast—the painful results of all of that madness between those three organizations, black men executed.

For the record, I want to make one thing clear about the whole black and white life experiences for me. I have met, worked with, and befriended a fair amount of white people in my life. Some who were very genuine, kindhearted, and the most generous human beings I have ever met in my life. They know who they are, I know who they are, and I did not forget about them. One name I will leave you with is Heather Heyer. A young woman who lost her life after being struck by a car in Charlottesville, Virginia, in the year 2017. She was standing up for what she believed in—standing up against racism, bigotry, and hate in this country. I hope one day, even if it is not in our lifetime, but I hope we can fix this whole black and white epidemic. But I hope and pray more that we fix this black versus black plague. It is as if black people are battling two wars at the same time. What is going on now is that we are living in this social media society. Where everyone is pointing their finger to other colors of people as if we are finger painting now, and not solving anything. If you are going to point your finger, make sure you use that same finger to pull people out of harm's way.

Apologies and reparations just will not cut it. The system of racism would have to be broken, unpracticed, and cease to exist. Another thing I want to say is this; when it comes to black people and white people. Why is it that we can be brothers and sisters, only when we are going through the same struggles, such as drug addiction, alcohol abuse, substance abuse, sexual assault, poverty, and things of that nature, but we cannot be brothers and sisters in winning? We cannot be co-founders or partners in business. When it comes to bad things, we are in sync with each other, but when it comes to the good, we are as divided as oil and water. That brings me back to my point about as long as the general white population does not need black people for employment or love, black people will always be the underdogs, we will always be treated as if we are beneath white people, and that we should always stay in that position.

One issue I believed that will always cripple us, black people, is seeking validation from the general white population. If a black actor only wins an NAACP award, but did not win an Academy Award, is that black actor satisfied with that? I am sure he or she wants that Oscar. Also, the whole phase with the hashtag "#Oscarssowhite." I thought that was very ignorant and childish, in my opinion. The real hashtag black people should have focused on is "#PRISONSSOBLACK." That should have been our topic to focus on and helping to reform innocent black men and women. But we so desperately want what white people have, and then cry protest when we cannot have it. You know, I love my people dearly, forgive me for saying this, but I think I would be accurate. I believe that if the devil himself placed a sign up in front of the gates of Hell, that says, "No Blacks

Allowed," there will be that one individual, that one black person, who would be outraged, who will protest and boycott Hell. That is how bad some people want what everyone else has. People want equality for everything; the good, the bad, and the ugly.

The day we were born on this earth, we received the highest award there is, the ultimate award, and that is being black. Why are we so obsessed, fiending for the general white validation? Us black people have tried too hard to be accepted and validated by the general white population, which, once again, does not need us for love or employment. For many years we have been wasting our precious time and money, consuming things of no actual value, for validation. We should not reduce our black excellence by posting the hashtag, "#blackexcellence," or "#BlackLivesMatter," because by doing so, all we get in return are people turning it into "#alllivesmatter," "#bluelivesmatter," and many other copycat hashtags. Our black excellence is much more powerful to be reduced to a hashtag. We show our black excellence by taking a knee, by having a dream, and by any means necessary.

How long do we as black people, expect our two thumbs to be our political activist? Posting away about social injustices in America. Social media is not giving us the solutions we need. Colin Kaepernick protested and lost his football career. By protesting on social media, the only thing you may lose is some followers. What are you willing to give up to make a difference? What are you willing to lose, to take the next needed stand?

Let me be very clear about this; there is absolutely nothing wrong with being who you are; as a white person, Asian, Middle Eastern, Latino, no matter your ethnicity or nationality. Always be proud of who you are. Yes, the history of white people was horrific towards other groups of people. My people, in particular, a horrifying, brutal history that can never be forgotten or fully forgiven, that was caused by white people. But that history does not have to define the person you are today. Nothing wrong at all with being white; be white, just do not ever be a racist, do not ever be prejudice, and you will be just fine. But to be fair, racism and hate are no longer just a black and white issue. It has become more diverse now. I have seen hate crimes such as black people attacking Asian people, young black people recording videos as they are brutally attacking homeless people. It is blacks, whites, Latinos, Asians, it is everyone. What did I say before? We have all done wrong, every ethnic group has done wrong in our society, but we can all do right! You see! I said, in the beginning, to come with an open mind and to read this with an open mind. Do we have work to do in America? Well, what do you think? By the looks of this whole political nightmare and the people who are in office now, yes, we have a long journey ahead of us in this country. Not just with the racism in America, but the racism worldwide.

One thing I want to say to my people who are on social media; our ancestors already knew what it was like not to be considered human beings. Our people have fought so hard and died for that privilege to be treated like a human being. As soon as we gained some of that human identity, we now have sacrificed it right back into the neighborhood of social media. I did not feel like a human being when I was on these platforms. I felt like just another n-word, "number," I mean. We are already so self-culturally prejudice towards ourselves. We assume and misinterpret what we say and become overly defensive. As I said before, instead of pointing the finger, use that same finger to pull someone out of harm's way.

I am not saying that I speak for every other black man, just like no other black man can speak for me. However, I feel that a lot of our issues are familiar because we are black men in a racist society, where we can relate negatively much more than we do positively. Because our collective problems are developed more negatively, we try to solve them with a negative solution, which is violence, gun violence, or on occasion, verbal and physical abuse—seeing two brothers or sisters challenging their intelligence for millions of views, when we should be collaborating our ingenious minds to form billion-dollar empires. But we just do not know how to confide in ourselves, with honor and loyalty. I just hope it is not too late.

13 *Likes*

Do You See What I See?

I know you might be thinking of the Christmas song, "*Do You See What I See*?" that is not exactly what I am referring to in this chapter. For the record, I do love that song; Johnny Mathis recorded my favorite version of it. What I am referring to is advertisements, articles, and news feeds. Everyone who is on these social media platforms, sees something completely different on their news feeds. From ads to daily news, articles, and our interests. When I was on social media, I would see these ads; ads that were somehow related to what I was searching for or looking up online. For example, I would look up clothes on yahoo or google. I would look for a turtleneck sweater or a pair of jeans. I would find the sweaters on multiple shopping websites. I would look at the catalog, and whether I purchased anything or not, I would exit out of the shopping sites and go back on social media. Then as I scrolled up and down my news feed, I would begin to see the same clothes that I was looking at on the shopping sites, except this time, it is an ad on social media.

I asked myself, "how the hell did my social media pages know I was looking at these clothes, or that new television, that new phone or video game? How did it know, or should I say who knew? It started to increase my paranoia, believing that a third party was watching me. Even when I think about a television show or a movie, and as soon as I would turn on the TV, I would see the same show or movie that I was thinking about at that moment. It is as if these smartphones and smart TV's can read our minds, a telepathic entity that can predict what we would be in the mood to watch. Perhaps we truly are living in parallel worlds, or just maybe we are being; watched. As if we are all in our little shows, like "*The Truman Show*," as I mentioned before. I must mention algorithms, which are very authentic as to why you see what you see.

Algorithms are what tracks down every step of activity you do online, especially on social media. Because of algorithms, we do not see or have the same news feeds. We never will. Algorithms need all the data and information they can get from you. Since it has been over a year that I escaped social media, I have no idea what these platforms have become. To help you better understand how algorithms work, I will give you an example; the Rubik's cube. With the Rubik's cube, you solve it by matching each side to the assigned color. So, to do that, you use multiple combinations of algorithms to solve one layer at a time. Then you solve the next layer, then the next, and finally match the top color. It is about knowing the combinations and color patterns, along with the formula of how to solve it. I know the algorithm formula by heart now, so, when I ever have a Rubik's cube, it is automatic for me.

Now with social media and the internet, whatever you happen to search for online, it knows what you recently searched for, and it creates these combinations of your searches. Whether that be shopping, news articles on Yahoo or Google, looking at your friends' profiles, or the videos you watch on YouTube. It documents any type of activity you do online, creates combinations and patterns of your online activities, makes predictions of your next moves to match what you will search for in the future, possibly. All of this just to keep you hooked, to keep you addicted, and to keep you consuming.

So, the more information and data you reveal, or should I say post and upload, the better these algorithms can predict who you are and what you like. It tries to match what videos you would like to look at; it matches which profiles you would like to see every time you open your social media accounts. Also, it knows when you have not logged on in a while. Remember when I said how the day I deactivated my FB; I was getting the repeated emails from FB saying how I was inactive on my profile and how I was missing out on so much? How is an app telling me that I am missing out on watching other people's personal lives? How does it know I am inactive?

Most importantly, why does it care? Why did it care that I was not logged on for some time? That is when I understood that we are being watched, always on these platforms. These platforms demand our "411," which is the code number for information, to those who do not know. Data is the most in-demand product in the world. Why do you think FB is a multi-billion-dollar company? Billions of people on social media, billions of photos, billions of posts, tweets, and stories.

Billions of webs of information and data that is being collected daily. Hour by hour, and minute by minute. Are you feeling lonely or sad? They know now. Are you related to this person? They know now. Are you in a relationship? They know! Everyone knows now. These platforms know so much about you that you barely know yourself anymore. You are just a puppet now. Every time you open one of these social media accounts, you see what they want you to see, and what they manipulate you to feel. You may believe you are in control, but you are being controlled; you are indefinitely being programmed. Scrolling up and down, seeing all these posts, you cannot stop yourself. Seeing one post; is just like a potato chip or a cookie; you cannot have only one.

Celebrities have it the worst. They are being watched exclusively. You would think that stars would be more cautious of what they post, but because the public eye is on them every day, the pressure is on. Celebs tend to lose it the most. Photos being leaked, six to seven-figure offers for pictures of their newborns; incredibly disturbing. But what I can say about celebrities; is that I do not see them as celebrities anymore. They are just human beings to me now. I have Kanye West to thank for that, and I will explain more about that in detail later on.

After quitting and deleting my accounts; and working with celebrities on television shows, I cannot see them the same. I stopped asking for pictures since there is no social media for me to post. I had no longer felt the need to ask for a photo with any of them, especially at this point in my life. Well, if I ever meet one of my idols, Denzel Washington or Will Smith, I will make an exception. But other than that, I stopped after I escaped the social media world. To be able to just look into people's eyes, celebrity or not, it has been better for me. I only treat people as people now. However, I do not think there is anything wrong with taking pictures of people or with celebrities. Still, sometimes people forget that stars are just as human as any of us, who need their space, and their privacy; if privacy even still exists in this world. We as human beings have this thing in our minds, something that contributes to both our dreams when we sleep and to our dreams for the future. We call it memories. Trust in your memories, you will still have those memories, as time goes by. Keep more things in mind than what you would post on your social media.

Getting back to what you see on social media, we see too much! They are not always pleasant things. You see the drags of humanity, all day long; watch out for this person, what out for that person, Trump this, and Trump that. They are giving people the inside scoop on fake news, just for them to spread rumors and create more drama. People are discussing and gossiping about things that have nothing to do with them. People are posting their opinions on social media, heated debates online, causing friendships to come to an end. Negative post has become more trending on social media, pulling more of people's attention, making much commotion online. Positive post tends to just relate to your real friends and family.

I would say try it to see for yourselves, but I rather you not. I am sure that you have already experienced half, if not all, of what I have experienced; the only difference is I am now on the other side of the fence. I can now see the disturbing manipulation and how addicted people are to social media. All the lies that you see. All of the rumors on other people's personal lives being told. Irrelevant information about who is dating who, who is the father of these celebrities' kids, or who is the wealthiest person in the world? Just so much information that is of no importance to your individual lives, your goals, and your dreams. Yet you are distracted by other's lives, other's looks, other's lies. There is definitely a type of method to this madness. I call this the C&C method: confusion and consumption. As I said before, the mind is a terrible thing to confuse, and these platforms are causing great confusion to the masses; and by the confusion you cause consumption. These third parties can just confuse your mind with mistruth, banking off of your naivety and ignorance, watch the increase of your paranoia, panic, and fear. They let you consume to whatever they want you consuming to at that moment. There are reasons why you cannot stop seeing ads from the fast-food chains.

Keep in mind that the real commercial is not on your television screen or your smartphones. The real commercial is right there in your gut; our hunger is the real commercial. It is the commercial we will feel every single day for the rest of our lives. The reason you see a McDonald's ad on television or social media so much; is because the company always wants to be your first choice to fulfill that hunger. They know you will be hungry every time you walk out that door, so while you are on your way to work, driving, or on public transportation, looking at your social media accounts, you will see their ads, over and over, until you consume. That is the new world we now live in, the social media world.

A world of likes, comments, views, followers of random strangers, fake profiles, fear, confusion, and consumption, this is simply not living. This is just sharing, posting, giving, stealing, denial, hiding, lying, basically, a nightmare. At least to me, it was. I shared things on social media that I probably should not have shared. I would "like" posts of certain things that I probably did not support, but I loved and cared about the people who posted them. I posted things that I did not truly agree with, but I knew it would draw some attention. I was that real person who became fake.

I became programmed just by getting with the program. The things that I would see in my news feed, the sudden anger I would feel and not know how to control myself. You ever had an argument with someone via text message or social media? Talk about showing your horns; I have had my share of both platforms, and I just hated myself for the things that I would say to people.

I felt that because the arguments were on a virtual basis, I did not have to take much responsibility for my words. But I was very wrong about that. Words can still hurt people, even if you are not saying them directly to a person's face. Sometimes it is hard to know when people are honest or sarcastic with their comments, and what kind of attitude or emotion lies beneath. The things we see in these screens; the ads, the politics, the third parties manipulating you, corrupting you, and your beliefs. That saying of, "if you want to hide something, put it in plain sight." Well, my addiction was in plain sight for twelve years, I was blinded by the likes, and distracted by the "woke" messages that I thought would help me. What saved me from these machines was to vanish from them entirely and disconnect from it all. I built up the courage to collect all of my pictures and post, screenshot them, and delete every last one until my profiles looked like an abandoned building or an isolated circus. As I said, I had to go through multiple pages before they finally allowed me to go free. The constant emails of telling me how I have not logged on in weeks; to catch back up with your friends who care about you. Making it through the "are you sure you want to delete your accounts? Are you really sure?" "Hell yes!" I am really sure! I was positive to log off!

You may be thinking that I am losing or missing out on meeting new people; perhaps I could have met the love of my life on social media by now. Maybe I could have posted something that made me go viral and been in Hollywood, living the actor's dream. The only thing I would be regrettably missing out on is life, my life. My life without the approval or validation of other people, my life without "likes," is the life I love. My life without scrolling around, looking at the lives of random strangers, has been a life of total bliss and salvation. My life has now been corrected; it has been humanized more than ever. Is my life perfect? Absolutely not! Does everything in life go my way? Not at all. Is my life easy to live? No, because life, in general, is a challenging trip we must take, and it will always have its bumpy ups and downs that we all must go through. Life will always have challenges to help us grow.

What I will say is that my life now is a life that I choose to live. My life is a life of patience, a life of treating others the way I would want to be treated. It is a life where I can call the shots. If I choose to stay in for the night, that is exactly what I will do. I do not have that fear of missing out on anything. I do not see other people partying, clubbing, traveling, marriage, and children. I reserve my time for what I value, and for who I value in my life. Even though I do not have dozens of people in my life, the people I do have in my life are the people who give me a genuine presence of respect, kindness, love, and care.

So, the question of do you see what I see goes deeper than you think. The real question I would like to ask you is, do you want to see what I see? Do you want to see what life is like on the other side of the fence? Do you want to see reality for what it is? That is what I will be sharing with you in the next chapter, what I see with my own two eyes, even my third eye if you believe in that. I see magic and mystery, nature like I have never seen it before.

Most importantly, I see myself. I know who I am, for the first time in twelve years. I know what I want to achieve in the future.

Hopefully, I can open your mind and present you with a different perception, a life without social media. Of course, I said this earlier, and I will repeat it right here; I cannot and will not tell you what to do with your life. By all means, do what is best for you, live your life, make your own decisions, and find your life lessons. That is how you grow and mature in life. It is alright; you do not have to make a decision cold turkey. It took me twelve years to understand this social media lifestyle was not for me. You may have individual businesses that you market via social media, which may undoubtedly help you, your brand, and your team development skills. There is nothing wrong with that.

If you are not bothered by comments, numbers, and have a real-life outside of your smartphones, that is wonderful, much success to you. But if you feel that something is not right, if you think that you are stuck or overly distracted in life, and social media has become more of a burden than a beneficial blessing, I am here to support your possible decision to take your leave. It is okay to escape it; walk away and never look back. Even if you just need a break for several months, as Jaron Lanier suggested, an intense six months. Just take time off of these platforms, heal your mind, and focus on what is essential for you. Focus on what matters in life for you, without the need for notifications lighting up on your smartphone every five minutes.

The overall purpose of me writing this book was not to tell you what to do or what is best for you. I do not know who you are. But what I would hope to achieve is that I give you a different outlook on life, especially if you are young and part of the new millennials who were born in the social media world. I just want to present you with another alternative. Present you with a different perspective, to see what life is like on the other side of the fence and see life the way God intended us to see it, with love and not "likes."

14 *Likes*

The Other Side of The Fence

I go through life now with purpose, with multiple purposes. I believe we have many purposes in our own individual lives, not just one. Perhaps that is why people become depressed about life so often, all over the world. People may believe they have "one" purpose in life, and that is it. People think we were born in this world with one purpose that they must pursue. That could be a singer, a professional athlete, or some kind of entertainer, and if they do not achieve their purpose, they feel as if they have lost in life. However, I actually believe now that we have more than one purpose in life. We can have multiple purposes to pursue in our lives, and that does not mean every avenue we choose to take, we have to become a millionaire. You can be more than an athlete, go above and beyond.

That is what I see now, by being on the other side of the fence. I see things differently; I see people differently, which is the most important. I find myself so patient with people now. I can be more open with people, having a good quality of conversations, without it becoming an argument or debate. I cannot recall when I last debated with someone. I just do not feel the need or value for debates. Not even with an argument, I tend to diffuse situations much more maturely and learned how to be in control of myself.

I talked about having more time on my hands since I deleted all of my social media accounts. However, that is just one of the perks I gained. I have increased both my listening ability and my ability to hear things; there is a difference between the two. I can hear the sounds of Miles Davis' music; I can hear the sounds of his horn better than I ever could hear it before and enjoy what I hear. I can listen to what people have to say, just listen. I do not argue with people; I allow them to speak fully, without cutting them off through mid-sentence, as I mentioned before. I respond and just be in the moment of the conversation. I do not even bother worrying about agreeing or disagreeing with people anymore. I believe that because of "social media," we love to hate other people's opinions. People cannot wait to disagree with each other, start up a commotion online. Next thing you know, people unfriended and blocked each other because of their difference in opinions. I do not have that issue with people as of now. In a conversation, there are no winners or losers. But hopefully, there are listeners.

I feel that people cannot listen to what others have to say anymore. People can hear when others are talking, but in their minds, people are thinking of the next thing they will say in a conversation and would not even wait for the other person they are talking with to finish; just cut them off. How can people change anything when they are not listening to one another? The lack of communication is at an all-time high. It is hard to have a full conversation with people without the interruption of a smartphone in today's world. I cannot recall the last time I was having a conversation with someone; without being distracted by the sudden buzzing of a phone. Whenever I go out now, I do not even think about putting my phone on the table. I had to deprogram myself and break that bad habit. There were times I would place my phone face up on the table so that I could see it light up whenever I received a notification. How quick it was for me to be distracted. But now, that bad habit is history. When I go out, my phone is in my pocket, on vibrate; and my full undivided attention is with whoever I talk with or interact with out in the real world. Of course, you may not think that is the case for you as an individual. But if you were to sit back and observe, I am sure you will see and then understand what I am talking about for yourself.

You may think that life would become too dull for you without social media, right? But I will tell you something; a year after I escaped social media, I did not realize how bored I was while I used those platforms. I even felt ashamed of myself that I dedicated the last twelve years of my young life to some meaningless likes, views, and followers. I will not say comments because I did appreciate the thoughtful and positive feedback from my friends, family, and others who I have met in life. But I really was bored with that lifestyle. Yes, it felt great when I posted it on social media. I felt like my opinions mattered more online, and they were instantly validated. But when I was not online; and had to step out into reality and be myself, I felt so empty inside, and I did not even know who I was.

You can use these platforms, but I do not believe you need them to succeed in life. They are just "show and tell," "post and delete," "I meant it- I apologize," applications. I am trying to do more in life than just being successful. Success is really for individuals to show off their achievements. But to win in life, that takes a team effort. I want to not only be successful but also to win in life. To create a team of people who are willing to achieve, just as much as I do, and win. I want to be successful, I want to win, and most importantly, I want to enjoy life. Embrace life, embrace the earth, and see the universe how God created it.

Life, on the other side, is rather beautiful. When I think about it now, I have no problem getting the much-needed rest at night. Because I am not on my phone at the wee hours of the night, and I do not have a bunch of random posts swirling through my mind. That was a killer for me. That was the cause of my anxiety for the longest. My anxiety and my thoughts just kept building up, as if I was on the last level of Tetris. I was staying up so late, looking at other people's lives, relationships, their problems, and their happiness. I do not know if I was happy for them, or sad because I wanted the same experiences as them. I would just stay awake and fantasize about my life being a different life. Then I had to come back to reality the next morning, with only three to four hours of sleep. Then before I even used the bathroom, I would open my phone and log back on to social media. I kept scrolling away, as if I did not stop.

That problem is solved now, thank God. More hours of rest, better sleep, better dreams, better mental health. A better life for me to live. A life with goals and ambition, without compromise. I can now go my own way, not needing the approval or validation of others. I see the world so differently. I see mother nature again. Nature is part of my life now; I no longer walk down sidewalks with my head down, scrolling up and down my phone. I have my head held up, and I can see reality, and do you know what I can see in reality? I can finally see Happiness; happiness is within reality. Happiness is within the sun, within the trees, the grass, the birds flying high in the sky; happiness is that experience. It is there, it has always been there, inside you; as I mentioned, it is a presence. All you have to do is declutter, remove the unnecessary things, and sometimes people who have no value to your life. Part ways with them respectfully, and then go on about your business. You do not owe anyone a friendship or relationship. We have those bonds with other people because we want to have them, we choose to have them. As I said before, you do not owe anyone a post into your life.

I realized that I did not owe anyone a piece of my life after a year went by. I do not owe anyone, and no one owes me. I do not have all the answers. I do not know everything; none of us know it all, even those who pretend to know everything. Even if you tried, what is the point to know about everything? If you already know everything, how could you learn anything? No one would be able to tell you anything.

To you, young people, if you are reading this and you are still in your teen years, or some of you are still a child. I beg of you, stop! Stop and think about what is happening. Stop and do some reflecting. I know this may be frustrating for you to understand at a young age. But if you please, figure out what it is that you want to achieve in your life. I know this will be a challenge because most of you younger ones, were born around the same time social media was born. Social media is like your older brother; it tells you what to do, what to think, feel, and how to behave. Find yourselves before you get seduced and sucked into this never-ending cycle of scrolling, posting, and double-tapping. I am sure you already know and heard that saying, "life is too short." Most of you who are reading this are probably teenagers. Look at how fast your childhood went by. It goes by so fast that it is heartbreaking; let me tell you. You do not want to dedicate those golden years to all of this technology, without committing your precious time to yourself.

I believe childhood is a shield of shining armor. Childhood is what young people must use to protect the man or woman they will choose to be in life. What do I mean by this? Well, as a child, you have the luxury to take this time and learn about yourself, learn who you are, and what you want in this life. Because of their youth, they are not, technically speaking, obligated to work and pay bills. They are not of legal age to deal with politics and voting if they are under eighteen. Being that many teenagers are under eighteen but who have social media accounts, these kids see some profoundly traumatic episodes of events that take place all over the world. I do not know what real impression social media brings on these young children. Just how you have to be legally eighteen to purchase cigarettes or be twenty-one or older to buy alcohol; there is no age requirement for social media. I believe these young ones, and some adults, have become undeniably addicted—the young ones, especially; because they are opening accounts at around thirteen years old. A naive teenage mind connected to these social media platforms is going to create some serious, uncontrollable social issues in our society. I see it every single day.

Let me tell you something else; here is another epiphany for you. Let's say we as human beings were genetically designed with the anatomy of having only one arm and one hand with fingers. The cigarette, cigar, the whole tobacco industry would have died a decade ago. You know why? Because people are so addicted to their phones and social media, they would have to decide to either hold and smoke a cigarette or hold and use their phones. These days you see way more people walking the streets with their phones in their hands; so, you be the judge of that. If you can imagine that, this is how addicted and enslaved we have become to these devices. You would probably forget you ever smoked, which would be beneficial to smokers; cut back on their health issues a bit.

I already know what some of you readers are thinking; you are probably thinking, "Well, I would just smoke first, and then get on my phone," or "I could smoke and hold my phone at the same time." Do you know how many cigarettes you would have dropped or have fallen out of your mouth? It would be so inconvenient and uncomfortable for you. Trust me, cigarettes would have died out a long time ago, if we humans only had one arm and hand. I think the porn industry would still survive, but that is for another book. But before I move forward, to all of the people out there with disabilities or arm amputees. Forgive me if this analogy came off uncomfortably; I am merely just making a point to how addictive these devices have become to our society.

But anyway, I strongly urge you; young people; to use this time of youth, for you, to get to know who you are, know what kind of people you want to make friends with; know about what interests you. Know about love and hate, happiness, and sadness. Because whether you wish to experience about both or not, you will experience both, and that is okay. As a child, you will need a great balance in life.

Keep this in mind; life does not define who you are; only you can identify who you are in life. If you are a low-key person, it is okay that you live a low-key lifestyle. If you are an outgoing type of person who loves some fun, exciting adventures, then that is the lifestyle you will live. It is just an unstoppable force of nature. Some of us had rough upbringings in life, yet we should not let those raw moments define or defeat us. Those are just what I had mentioned before; moments of victimization that some of us experience. But please, do not be seduced by that victimization. Do not allow the victimization to manifest your destiny.

Life belongs to no one; it is just a physical, real moment of mystery, that we all must live through. Life is truly just an experience. Life is life, and you are you. So, you go out there in the world to be who you are; in this thing called life. Money does not define you; materialism does not represent you, and neither does the number of likes, comments, views, followers, or subscribers. You are more divine than all of those human-made sources of validation.

Find your passions, whatever that may be for you. I like to think of this idea of the word "career." I do know the definition of the word career, of course. However, when I look at this word, I cannot help but to separate the letters and see the word "car." So, the next time you think of the career you want to have in life, figure out what exactly "drives" you. Metaphorically speaking, what drives you to achieve great things in life and what drives you to success. What will motivate you to win? Do not choose a career that will drive you crazy if you are fortunate enough to have a choice.

I was lucky to have help in choosing my career as an actor. When I was a freshman in college, I was filling out this application for a scholarship, but I needed two letters of recommendation. So, I asked my business professor, Dr. McHugh, for a letter of recommendation. Then I asked this great man by the name of Devon, who was my financial aid advisor. One night I was at a basketball game on campus, I ran into Devon, and we were having a conversation. Devon brought up this audition for this play called "The K-Word," which was a stage reading play, based on some survivors of hurricane

Katrina. Devon wanted me to get involved with some of the activities on campus; I said no, absolutely not.

I never acted before, so for me, being a shy and quiet kid, I would have never had the courage or nerve enough to perform in front of a live audience. I said no again, and then Devon said humorously, "*alright, if you do not audition, I am not writing the recommendation.*" What a great way to get blackmailed, right? But for some reason, I wanted to finish this scholarship application, which I did not end up getting anyways. So, I went along and auditioned for the play. I got a role in the play; did four shows, I believe. After that play, I knew this is what I wanted to do for the rest of my life. Being on that stage, that commitment, that focus that is much needed, the love I have for it, and still have it inside me to this day. It changed my life forever.

Acting as a professional is one of my passions. It is my drive to success and winning. I was eighteen when I started, had some ups and downs along the way. But for me now, it is just the beginning. As I said before, to succeed in life is more of an individual based mission. But to win, you need a team of people. For example, if a man or woman is morbidly obese, and then loses a lot of weight, that person has succeeded. If a team of people came together to create a workout and dietary plan that helps and saves the lives of thousands of obese people, that team has won. But here is the thing; it is possible to be both successful and to be a winner. Success can be overcoming personal issues, such as addictions, which is what I achieved. Winning would be the love and support from your family, the teamwork that you need to keep you on the right track.

That is how I look at both success and winning. By escaping the social media world, for me to log off and go my own way, I have become one of the most successful people in the world. At least that is how I feel on the inside. Now, I am ready to win in life. I am prepared to see life the way it is supposed to be seen. With respect, with appreciation, with love and, most importantly, for many purposes. Let me say again; we have many purposes in our own individual lives, not just one. Believing that we have only one purpose in life, we choose to dedicate our entire lives to that one purpose. If that one purpose does not fall through, we then start to live with everlasting regrets. Which then creates the crankiness, the fearfulness, the paranoids, the negativity, and the hopelessness. Then those same people who failed at their one purpose; they tell children that they will not succeed, that the kids will fail as well, which will then encourage children to quit before they even try. Those are the same people who are hiding behind those profiles, writing such horrible things on other people's pages; the "catfishes."

The challenge is to expand your mind, and then find those purposes; patiently. Just like kids in school, their purpose in school is not to learn only one subject. Students must learn about English, history, mathematics, music, and so on. We have created a society that minimizes our vision when we should maximize our vision and reduce the consumption of mundane things. In the future, we can, and we will expand our minds and expand our purposes.

Life on the other side of the fence is only going to get better for me. No, my life will not be perfect; it will have it upsetting moments, but at the very least, I will not look at life as a colossal disappointment. I now look at life only as life. I now see people as who they are, just people. Just human beings ready to take on their challenges for the day. I look at life with a moving forward journey now. When one door closes, I prepare for another one in the future. There are times when you have to be aggressive about your purposes, maybe even a little selfish. But that comes with the territory of succeeding and winning. Risks are meant to be taken, so take them. Take risks, but do not take people for granted. Do not take spending time with people for granted. If you make time to see people, try to stay committed to that! I believe that is one of the reasons why social media has ruined friendships. Because we see our friends on social media all day long, in our minds, we might say, "Oh, I will just see my friends another time. I already know what they are doing through social media, and I will just "like" a few of their pictures to show and send my love."

Social media has become a virtual ocean of millions of ships. Not actual ships such as cruise ships, but friendships, relationships, partnerships, and companionships. All these ships are sailing away; some that crashed so suddenly, hitting those icebergs that I call debates and broken promises; and eventually watching them founder, deep within. It is better to just have real friends, in real life, that you spend real time with and create the special moments and memories for you to remember forever. Friendships and relationships cannot grow and blossom from you planting a seed, by following someone on social media, and then just water that seed with the sprinkles of likes. It takes great effort to make real friends in this life, in this world.

I just find it so funny now. I would never have thought with the things I have seen online, that I would see people make an absolute fool of themselves. Make a fool of their families, just for a little attention, for a bit of fame. Fame and attention are going to destroy and kill talent for good. I believe that social media is the Hollywood, that Hollywood never was. Social media is "Netflix," and Hollywood is slowly becoming "blockbusters." Why do you think Hollywood constantly make deals with social media sensations? Why do you think entertainers feel the need to use these tools to maintain their careers? Hollywood is trying everything in its power to stay relevant in this social media era, especially with the actual "Netflix" and "YouTube" community. I say this because if you want to find entertainment, you no longer have to go to the movies, you could just pull out you phone, and you are good to go. Pretty soon, skill and ability will be a thing in the past. It will only be about your following on social media. It is so crazy how people will respect you more, based on a number from an app.

Another thing that comes to mind that Jim Morrison said was, "this is the strangest life I've ever known." Jim has been gone for over forty-eight years now, yet he was way ahead of his time. With the knowledge and wisdom, simply way ahead of this time. Because the life I see now through my eyes, seeing everyone on those phones, on social media, I agree; "this is the strangest life I have ever known!" I fear that it will get even more bizarre.

I remember seeing a father with his two sons, coming into a pizzeria to have dinner one night. I was waiting for my order to come out. I remembered the father sitting down with his sons and hearing the father say, "*alright guys, the first rule of business; no cell phones.*" One of his sons listened and put his phone away swiftly, but the other was hesitant. He was refusing to put his phone away. The son was playing a game, and the game damn near possessed that son. He could not put his phone down; even after his father repeatedly told him to put his phone away. The son kept saying, "Hold on! Hold on! Wait!" Those sons had to of been no older than ten or eleven. If they were addicted to their phones at that age, I could not even imagine what their lives are going to be like once they hit high school.

What is there to come for the youth in the next five years? In ten years? Twenty? The pain will happen to them, like an unexpected flu. The pain from cyberbullying, kids seeing their friends on social media, who they have not talked to in a while, hanging out with new friends, having a great time, and feeling like they are missing out. The youth feeling pain from not having enough. Not enough likes, followers, subscribers, or views. Well, enough is enough.

What I learned after seeing life on the other side of the fence is this; you do not have to be special to live a special life. You do not have to be a celebrity, rich or famous, with luxurious things, to say you have made it in life. To live this so-called "American Dream." Yes, there will be painful times, but when it comes, we just have to walk ourselves through it, sing through it, dance through it, hug it through, and sometimes cry it through.

If you were to try this different lifestyle, just try to live your life without social media for a while, without looking at your phone every five minutes because of boredom. To see what your life will be like, on the other side of the fence. You will see the magic of life again, the wonders and mysteries of it all. You will see yourself the way you have never seen yourself before. You will feel alive again! You can just have your own life to live without the validation of random strangers that you will never even get to know. If you can find yourself one day, living your life without it because you see no value in these platforms anymore. You have my full support and understanding. You will be able to appreciate the life you already have. Just watch; if or when you take time away from social media, you will wake up one morning, stretch your body, and just lay in bed for ten to fifteen minutes. You may find yourself staring up at your ceiling, just thinking. You would not even think about touching your phone.

Your mind will be at ease. You would be able to self-reflect, clear your mind of any distractions, begin to think natural positive thoughts again. No likes, no comments, no new followers, and the only views you would need is the views you see with your own two eyes. You will find yourself again; then, in finding yourself, you will get to know yourself better than you ever have known yourself before. It is essential to be educated on many things in life. Still, the most crucial part is knowing the education of self. Educate yourself on who you are as a person, man, woman, child, as a human being, knowing what is right for you.

If you feel that social media is for you, by all means, proceed. Again, I am not here to tell you what to do—just presenting a different perception, a different point of view. I get it; social media has a way of keeping you in the loop of everything. But look at how people are treating each other on these platforms. There is barely any love there. You see adults on social media behaving like children, temper tantrums. Instead of talking face to face, conversating like adults, you see grown men and women posting videos going back and forth with each other. People Arguing about personal situations that are not for the world to know about. All those foolish hashtags, all the counter-attacks. I cannot imagine what kind of impression this is doing to the youth. Kids see everything; as I said before, this is really an adult world.

We have to get our minds focused on what is important. We must first make the minds of people a better place to store knowledge and information, and then we can make the world a better place, one day at a time. Another thing about that is this; I get tired of hearing people say that when our loved ones die, they are in a better place. Not that I disagree that they are in a better place, but we should not wait until we die to have that better place. We have to make this world a better place starting now. Otherwise, these younger generations of children are no longer going to appreciate or have value for life on earth. They will just want to go straight to that better place. To them, the earth will just be the middleman that they want to cut out.

Social media has corrupted our values, contaminated our minds with false information, negativity, producing mood swings, and provoking lousy behavior. It Feeds people's minds with poisoned perceptions and hopelessness. Keep in mind, the earth does not need us to survive, we need the planet for us people to survive, and we have to get with setting it right for the new generations to come. Educate the youth on how to take care of themselves and have a future. Not to have people focus on having a career based on how many likes they accumulate on these apps.

I mean, yes, we as people have sung and recorded some amazingly immaculate songs. We have made some unforgettable movies and painted some pictures that showed the times and era we lived in, once upon a time. We are simply guest on this earth, just here to make some memories. If we keep going with this routine of uploading all of our precious memories, our photos, our artwork, and ideas to our accounts, just for likes and attention; we will not have anything left in our minds to hold; that is sacred and private. This behavior will lead us to not having the ability to have a functional thought process. Polluting our creative juices and lose our social skills that were once respectable. If nothing is changed, if people do not change, these platforms are going to produce millions of empty minds.

People are seeking information to store not in their minds, but saving it in their phones and on their social media profiles. They are allowing these empires to collect all of your data and memories.

I can see it clearly, a hundred years from now; a grandparent is getting their grandchild ready for bed, and the grandchild wants their grandparent to tell a story about what life was like; when their grandparent was a kid. The grandparent would not have a clue in their brain, because everything was captured and uploaded to their phones, iCloud, or God knows what else will be around at that time. So then, that grandparent would have to get their phone and say, "Hey Siri, create a slideshow of my childhood." That could be freighting; perhaps it is too soon to believe this could be the world a hundred years from now. (On a side note, I proofread out loud, as I proofread this book, and every time I said, "Hey Siri," my iPhone kept responding, saying, "I'm here! These smartphones, I'll tell you).

Again, I am not automatically assuming that you are addicted to social media like I once was. As I said, you may have no problems using these platforms. You may even love social media; it may be your bread and butter, the best thing that ever happened to you. But just understand this; success does not come so frequently. Social media is too fast, too advanced for reality. One good thing happens to you; you get a ton of likes, then when the likes fade out, you will always be thinking about what the is next thing you have to post. What is the next success story you will have to post after the last post went viral?

I swear; for the years I was on social media, on my smartphones; my two thumbs turned into Bevis and Butthead. All of that scrolling, hitting the like button, commenting on stranger's pages, it was a real waste of my time, a sincere regret.

But now, that is all gone. I have not touched that like button in well over a year. I have not double-tapped on my smartphone screen and saw that big heart icon, showing up in front of the post. Talk about life-changing; logging off created a different connection with other people for me. To not pass judgment on people, to respect their differences, and just for me knowing more and more about myself every day, there is no need for likes in my life now. There never was a need for them. You do not need "likes" when you already love yourself, remember that.

As I said, I did not have anyone to help me with my social media addiction. I did not know who to turn to for help. I had no solution to put an end to it. I realized my only solution was to delete my accounts and escape this nightmare for good, so that is what I did. One by one, I removed each profile. After I deleted them all, I felt like I boarded on a spaceship and shot off to the Moon or Mars. At first, I felt so alone, but only at first. As time was going by, I was getting stronger, mentally. Then when I saw Jaron Lanier on "The View," when I read his book, I suddenly understood that I was not alone, and that felt great. It felt like I had some support, and I was happy about that.

So, now you know where I stand with everything. For the rest of my life, I am not using these things anymore. God willing, I live to be a hundred and twenty-five years old, you will not see a profile of me on these platforms we have now, and the platforms to come in the future. I want to experience the life that God had designed for us to experience. A life of discovery, travel, looking up at the sun and the moon, a life of embracing and appreciating our existence on this earth. I found that in me; over this past year and made some exciting discoveries about myself. I learned that I am a good man, a good human being, and proud to be of African descent. I am not a perfect man, but I learned that a life without social media is perfectly fine. I learned that if I can overcome an addiction, and if I can escape this nightmare and make my life a better life, I can do anything of good cause.

I am not a celebrity. I understand that my word for it may not be as valuable to you. That my experience with social media maybe not be as convincing to some who would read this. But trust me; no one is immune to addictions, which is why I had to make a life choice not to drink alcohol, and not indulge in drug use. I took it a step further by living on a plant-based diet and escaping the western food that will eventually kill us all; slowly but surely.

Again, I am not perfect, and you are not perfect, no of us are. However, that does not mean we should not go down that road to evolution. To continue to grow and mature, and leave behind things that were once fun, but then became toxic. Flings can be enjoyable when you are young. But as you get older, they will become toxic, and you will want to be more exclusive with your relationships. Well, some of us will, at least.

I wish I could erase a lot of things from my mind that I had seen on the internet and social media before I deleted everything. That is not to ignore those disturbing incidents I saw on social media. But by observing these tragic events, over and over, and knowing I could not do anything about them after I had seen them, it was merely the scrolling of heartbreak. A heartbreak that I was too numb to feel. Seeing the news feeds of negativity and all of these mass shootings, people recording fights, racial profiling, and the list goes on. To view this every single day; of course, this will drive people mad, make them paranoid, a whole new wave of conspiracy theorists, and parents being so afraid to send their children to school. This is not living; this is a living hell.

The only question that I have is this; what does the world want? Not the earth, but the world? The planet will take care of itself regardless; it has been doing so for billions of years. The world, however, as we know it, what are we as people, going to do about our lives? Just to leave money behind for your children is simply not good enough. We have to leave behind the knowledge of survival, how to appreciate, and how to create. Also, to practice the pursuit of prevention. Technology is of convenience, a luxury. But to create something to maintain and protect life, not just human beings, but animal life, plant life, life across the board; that is where we need to focus; forever.

I do ask myself how all of this happened? How did I become addicted to a social media app? Then I answered that question myself; I am only human. That is how this happened to me. Some people are addicted to alcohol, addicted to drugs, cigarettes, sex, pills, opioids, and also food. To repeat, I do not drink alcohol, and I do not smoke or do drugs. So, what was my vice going to be? That vice found me through social media and had me hooked for twelve years. What I hope you learn from this book is that you are only human. It happens to the best of us; addictions I mean. We lose ourselves in these addictions, and we lose the love for ourselves. So, do not soak your spirit in the waters of shame or disappointment; just because you let yourself down by not being in control of yourself and becoming addicted.

You, as a person, as a human being, are worth much more than the number of likes, views, and followers. I say this again and again because I want you to believe that. I want you to keep that in mind. To the young ones, your life is worth so much more than the world is showing you right now. But you must see that with your own two eyes first. Your presence, your existence on this earth, is appreciated, even if you have not yet met many people who will understand you. We all want to be loved. But from my experience, I believe that social media has created a false narrative that manipulates you into thinking millions should like you; and if you do not fulfill a certain quota of "likes," you take that as being unloved. These machines have reduced everything about our character. We are so focused on going viral and would be willing to do just about anything to make that happen, even commit a crime, a murder.

Life, on the other side of the fence, has protected me from that manipulation. The fake news that can no longer invade my mind and confuse me, to see people without prejudice. To walk in Manhattan, from thirty-fourth street, all the way to Lincoln center, and not be engaged in my phone. Yet that is all I see now; I see thousands of heads looking down at their phones, thousands of glowing blue-lit faces walking around Times Square. The eyelids, remember?

To see people not paying attention to where they are walking, so hypnotized by their phones. As I said, I did feel alone in the world when I first logged off of social media. The world looked so strange to me. I felt like this alien on another planet, another time. When I escaped, when I deleted my accounts, I was taking the red pill. I remembered standing in Times Square, observing my surroundings. I begin to realize that I was on the outside looking in; I was looking at the Matrix. People have become mentally enslaved by these six-inch machines in the palm of their hands—these machines that are with us every step of the way, daily. My God, these machines even count how many steps we take.

To be honest with you, I saw the movie "*The Matrix*," for the very first time several months ago. The movie came out in the year 1999; I was only nine years old. I would not have understood what the movie was trying to explain to its audience at that young age. So, I am glad that I saw this movie as a man, a much wiser man. I know the Matrix; I see it every day. Whether I see it on the television, online, through emails, billboards, or seeing ads on social media every time I opened my profiles. The Matrix is just everywhere. There are ads for everything; toothpaste, furniture, fast food empires, pharmaceutical companies, surveys, basically every trick in the book to pull you into consuming. The craziest thing about these social media platforms is that they do not even require us to pay for it with money. The only way you pay for it; is by paying attention, giving these machines all the attention, as much time as it can get from every one of us. It wants our data, it wants our energy, it wants our minds, it wants our fears, it wants our Gods, and it wants our souls.

Now that I think about the Matrix. We have become batteries to these platforms. Since these services are free, the only way that they are meaningful, is by us human beings, giving it our time and our energy. The average human life span is between 75 to 100 years old. You are looking at social media, with a battery life that lasts for over seventy-five years, with younger generations to keep it alive as they are born. Remember what I said about seeing infants holding on to these phones for dear life? Social media is just getting started. That energy is not just for social media; that is for our jobs, companies selling products, athletics, basically everything that requires the energy from human beings. I think I understand now; more than ever, that scene where Morpheus was holding up the battery. We, as human beings, are being reduced to batteries that charge these social media platforms, every single day. That is something to think about, but by no means should you take it literally.

You may think that life is non-existent on the other side of the fence. In all honesty; Life is heaven on Earth. Being off of this stuff, it will make you feel like Julie Andrews walking on the mountaintop singing, "*The Sound of Music*." I do not believe you will miss out on crucial opportunities. I told you; I was on social media for twelve years, and not once did I ever receive an acting role or audition via social media. Everything I have achieved in the film and television world, I earned through hard work and dedication. Social media was just the platform for me to boast and brag about it. If you want something, get on out there and get it. Do not wait for a social media app to tell you that you are qualified, based on the number of followers you have. Do not break your back, trying to go viral for views.

Do not waste anymore of your time. Again, if you know what is best for you, if you know social media is what keeps your brand, your business alive, please proceed. However, if or when these machines stop, what are you going to do? What will happen if or when your data, information, precious memories stored on these devices and apps suddenly disappear? Will that event really be our doomsday? Will that be Armageddon? I would hate for that to happen.

The bottom line I would like to make is, do not make social media the end all be all of your life. I did not know any better about getting off these apps before. I wish I did when I was a teenager. My life would have been different if I was not on them. Once again, I do not paint myself, nor do I see myself as a victim now. I was just a young curious kid, using this new digital toy. A smart toy that ended up using me.

You will have better days if you decide to take a break, at the very least. Relax your consciousness, draw your focus more towards your own life, and not the presence of random strangers. Devote more time to your actual family and real friends. Also, for God's sake, if you are out on a date, for the love of God, put your phones away. I am sure whoever you are on a date with, you were texting each other excessively before meeting up for that date. Why go on a date just to sit there, both of you on your phones, scrolling around social media? You both might as well have stayed home, and face timed each other eating a meal.

It would be a massive step for you if you were to come over on the other side of the fence. It will feel weird at first like I said earlier. But being a human being is kind of funny. We have so many differences from other living species; we are continuously evolving. I just feel that we are developing more and more into zombies, rather than better people. Young people, if you are looking to follow someone, follow me! One of my favorite Tupac songs, "*Hail Mary*;" at the beginning of this song, he says the words, "*follow me*!" His voice and energy when he said those words are how I relate it to you when I tell them to you, "follow me!" Come with me; escape this dead-end lifestyle while you are still young enough to catch it. Catch this message that I am sending to you, change your behavior, and I promise you, you will see life for what it truly is, alive and beautiful.

One final thing in this chapter that I would like to touch on briefly; I know that there are people out there; older people and younger people who are waist-deep in depression; sinking their way into suicidal thoughts. One of you could be reading this. I just want to say to you, "STAY WITH US!" Stay here with us; you have many great purposes on this earth to live and experience through. You may not see or know what your purposes are right away. You may not know who you are just yet. You may feel stuck. But trust me when I say this to you. You earned your right to be here on this earth, just like everyone else. No, you may not fit the standards of beauty that our biased society has unfairly required.

You may not have been blessed with many financial means in your family, and yes, life may have hit you hard; from a very early age. But you must keep swinging. You must keep fighting; keep moving forward and keep on breathing. Keep on keeping on, as my former professor would say, who is a great friend and mentor of mine to this day. Your existence is exquisite. Think about it; you were in a race with hundreds of millions of other sperm cells, racing to your mother's egg. You are the one; you are a success. You out swam over a half a billion sperm cells to reach the finish line; to the promised land. You already won in life by being born. No matter what job you land in this life, no matter if it does not pay you as decently, you are not a loser. You are not inferior. As I said; nothing that can hire you or fire you can define you; you represent you. You may not always be the wisest person, but you can be the bravest. You may not always be the best looking in the room, but you can be the strongest.

We go through hell at times in our lives. I had experienced that feeling. Not a sense of suicidal thoughts, but a feeling of giving up. A feeling that everyone I would meet in life; would just turn on me or leave me, betray me because I felt I was not good enough. Until I grew a pair of you know what and said to myself, I am enough for me! I am enough for myself, the hell with the validation of random strangers, the hell with social media, and the manipulation games that it plays with us. I said to myself that my life, my dreams, are mine to protect, and not to post. So, I beg those whoever thought of taking their own lives or anyone else's life for that matter; I ask you to take a look at your own life; find your purposes, not just one purpose, but multiple purposes, and find your balance. Discover your good, discover your bad, and see you. Do not worry about bullies; chances are; bullies are the ones who are being bullied.

You are not helpless, and you are not hopeless. It is not too late for you to escape and come back to reality. Lift your heads out of your phones and let the world see your faces. Let the world see your eyes and not your eyelids. Whenever you are ready, come over to the other side of the fence. It is alive, it is beautiful, and your existence on this earth is not followed or defined by numbers. But determined by the person you are on the inside, identified by your humanity.

15 *Likes*

The Past, the Present; the Future?

Twelve years is a long time. To be logged on to social media without a break, it does its' damage. I would not consider myself a hundred percent healed from my addiction. I do not believe that I will fully recover from my social media addiction. I feel that if I were to ever go back on these things; my addiction would be waiting right there for me; with flower emojis and heart-shaped likes saying, "welcome back, I missed you." I realized that logging off was going to be a lifetime commitment, no turning back. It is just like a drug addiction. You cannot take a break from drug addiction, then relapse and think you will be able to control it. It is the same situation with alcohol. You cannot take a break from something that has already broken you. It will just cut you more and more; until you are in pieces that cannot be placed together again.

It was simple; this lifestyle was not working for me. So, I had to take my leave from it all. It was not about pointing the finger to anyone, blaming someone for my addiction. How do you blame someone before you blame yourself? I figured out that I had a problem, and the only way I was able to solve it was by leaving it all behind me and never look back. I exchanged numbers with the people I wanted to stay in touch with; I did my last post thanking everyone for my birthday wishes; said goodbye, and that was it. I left for good. I said goodbye to the likes, new friend requests, and new followers. Goodbye to those silly games and party invites. It was no more opening up my phone every two minutes. After twelve years, it was so life-changing for me.

So, to recap everything I do not do in my life; I do not have social media, I do not eat animal products, I do not drink alcohol, do not smoke, no drugs. You may be asking, "what in the hell does he do with his life? No more vices? I will say this one last time; I am not perfect. The man I am today took a lot of hard work to achieve; and a lot of time. I had to make decisions and live by those decisions; to make my life a better life to live. I did not want to live miserably; I refuse to live that way. You can either worry about the things you cannot control and be miserable or concentrate on the things you can change. Take the other direction in your life and go far. The choice was up to me, just like the choice is up to you. Now, of course, I am not trying to convince you to go vegan or stop smoking or drinking if you do. That is for another book. The choice to let go of social media is up to you as well. You know where I stand with it all by now. But that does not mean you have to feel the same. Of course, you do not even have to agree with me. Keep this in mind; many of the innovators, the leaders of Silicon Valley, do not allow their children to use these social media products and services; think about that.

If I did not believe that there was a problem with these platforms, if I did not think I was addicted to social media; trust me when I tell you; I would not have written this book. I would still be logged on, scrolling my life away, looking for attention, giving attention, and losing my real character. But this was a problem for me; I was addicted, and I hated it. I did not like the man that I was on social media. Social media is where my manhood started. Again, I started social media when I was sixteen years old; I grew up on all of it, and it contributed to the man I was becoming. The man I was becoming was misinformed, naïve; I would even say cowardly. I would wait to make first impressions to a woman on social media, rather than just cutting the middleman out and talking to a woman in person.

That was another thing too, seeing women on there every day. Women that I felt for; desired. Women who I felt could have been the one for me. The more and more I scrolled and saw them, the more profound the fantasy of being with them grew inside of me. But that fantasy was continually being destroyed by reality. It just came to the point where every time I saw them on social media, the women that pulled me in, the anxiety would shoot through my body. It would shock my body, I would be unable to breathe, mainly if those women would entertain other men. That is when it all hit me; on these social media platforms, I was becoming a boy again. It contained my ignorance and immaturity. A real man would not entertain or feed into this nonsense.

To be honest with you; this year without social media, is the first year of my life, that I have my authentic manhood. I have my courage now. The masculinity that is under my control; manhood that I choose to mold and prep for the future. Not a manhood that is reduced to boyhood, going on rants, and posting them to social media. The man that I am today is the man that I have been searching to be for a long time. Would you find it strange or conceited if I considered myself a hero of my own? Because I believe that should be one of our purposes in life. By taking the time to know yourself and find yourself, you then create the potential of being a hero of yourself, being your personal God. Not being "the God," the creator of course; but being your own God, in a way where you love yourself more, take care of yourself, your body, and the planet. By not reducing yourself to anything less.

Social media was crippling me, crippling my potential to be something great, to be a good human being. These devices; these services are taking over your minds, playing with your brains like a yo-yo. Changing your moods every day, getting you to do anything it wants you to do, and telling your intentions to record this, record that.

I get it; we as human beings love imagination. Our minds are driven by imagination. We cannot help but be addicted to imagination and fantasy; while we completely ignore and escape reality. That is why we love Walt Disney Pictures and Disney World so much. It is escapism from reality. The music, the movies, the cartoon characters could put a smile on anyone's face, from infants to the elderly. What social media did was it allowed everyone to create their character, a real-life avatar, that we can create a whole life for in the palm of our hand. The character uses our image, our flesh and blood, and most importantly, our time.

We can create our own fairy tale world on these platforms; create many illusions that we would believe to be true. Random people commenting on your page, telling you that you are the biggest inspiration; they love you; they want to be you. That is going to feel significant to you. But all it takes is one bad comment or one bad day. All it takes is one person to call you fat, ugly, fix this, fix that. That is when you are brought back to reality. You will always see them slithering around your post and comments, like some rattlesnake, ready to attack you. Miserable people will never disappoint you.

But yes, we are captivated by our fantasies, I understand. Social media is fantasy land like we've never seen it before. All of your favorite childhood companies have accounts on social media. It is just everywhere; I see the little social media icons on so many products in stores. You see the social media icons on a bag of chips, candy bars, cookies, coffee cups, even packages of diapers. It is the world we live in, a world where everyone has a price, and everything has an ad.

There is something that I envisioned some time ago; that I feel is eerily possible in the future. Since I mentioned imagination, can you imagine one day; deceased people having their social media profiles engraved on their tombstones? Where people could go to visit a loved ones' grave, and the deceased person's "@ names" would be engraved on their tombstone. People would be able to take their highly advanced smartphones of that time, scan the headstone. What will then appear on their smartphone, the social media profiles of that deceased person. People could see who other people once were, what their lives were like, who was or is a family member of these people, when, and how they died.

In a way, that could actually be a beautiful thing. If that were a possibility one day; there could be generations of people, who would visit their ancestor's graves; ancestors who have been deceased for centuries; have their relatives scan their tombstones and see what their ancestors looked like when they were living. Hell, people could be adopted and research their biological parents. If their biological parents are no longer living, those adopted children can visit their biological parent's grave. Parents who they never met and get to see them for the very first time, just by scanning their social media platforms that were placed on their headstones. It sounds so over the top right? But I see that possibly happening one day, where people will want to be remembered, either so desperately or sacredly. They would engrave their full name and social media accounts on their headstones instead of engraving their birth date and date of death. Even after their death; those people will still want you to see their profiles and remember them that way. If the Kardashian family does not do this first, I am sure some other famous people will. I will go even further; there may not be headstones in cemeteries in the future.

I see holograms of the deceased replacing headstones. Imagine a family going to the grave of a loved one, who is now a hologram. Being greeted by this holographic loved one who has now passed away. The hologram can say hello to the family. It knows their names, asks how their life is going, and the hologram telling its' loved ones; "Please don't cry. I will always be with you; I will always love you."

Remember what I said earlier about one day the innovators of the future could invent a new smartphone? A smartphone that could take a snapshot of a newborn baby; and potentially predict how it will look by the age of fifteen? Well, tragedies do occur, unfortunately. There are the unfortunate times, where new parents lose their newborn babies; to many different causes. One of them being "sudden infant death syndrome." God forbid that happens in the future, but if that were to occur, unfortunately, and the parents would have to bury their infant child, this one day, could be a healing alternative. Let us say that this possible new smartphone and hologram; would be able to come together and create a concept of this newborn baby who has passed away. As time goes by, this new smartphone and hologram would then create the illusion of that infant child, growing up. With these new tech machines, the smartphone, and the hologram, that infant child would grow into a little kid, then into a teenager, and then into an adult. The parents of that deceased infant child could visit its grave from time to time, check-in, and see their son or daughter, growing up virtually. Think about it if you can; the parents being able to see their deceased infant child; crawling, taking their first steps, because of these new tech machines. Even holographic animals; pet cemeteries, where owners could play fetch with the hologram of their deceased dogs.

I do not know if that would be possible or even sane. But the truth is, you just never know what will happen in the future. One could imagine; driving down a highway at night. A road that is next to a cemetery; filled with thousands of these glowing blue holograms of the deceased. These holograms would be walking around the graveyard, greeting each other, at peace with themselves. I know this all sounds insane to live in a world like that. But the way technology is now, five hundred years from now, when we are all gone, that could be us. We just may certainly be those holograms—walking around greeting each other. Think of the celebrities of that futuristic time, who then passes away. People then could visit their grave and take a selfie with their favorite celebrity hologram. You just never know.

I would even see social media having a future feature, where you can store a posthumous post. So, the way this feature would work is when a person dies, their profile will automatically post the pictures they saved in their posthumous file, sporadically. Just so that keeps people engaged with their profile and their memory for a long time. Of course, the ads will be right there. Remember, as I said earlier, in the future, there may be smartphones that can predict our deaths. Let's say, for example, someone dies of a heart attack. Then their smartphone or smartwatch will notify their social media profiles and declare them deceased by the heart attack. Later on, social media apps will begin the process of their posthumous post. Then with their posthumous post comes an ad for a new pharmaceutical pill that could potentially save your life from a heart attack. It all sounds so bizarre right now, I understand. But this is what could happen in the future. It could be the new way of life all over the world—an unforgettable world, where nothing or no one will ever be forgotten, even after death.

God knows what will happen fifty to a hundred years from now with these platforms, and the new social media sites to come. I even look at a thousand years from now. Where a smartphone or smartwatch controls everything, perhaps there will be smart glasses, where people who are legally blind can put on these smart glasses, and the smart glasses will guide the blind through their everyday lives. They will have a Bluetooth activated earpiece attached to the glasses; that will help those legally blind people with voice-activated GPS walking directions. The glasses would help them with information, daily reminders, and perhaps describe in detail, the environments the legally blind people are walking in at the moment. The Siri-like voice would explain to the legally blind person the date and time, what the weather looks like for the day, everything, even how many likes and views they gained on their last post.

Could you imagine in the future, people wearing solar panel baseball caps? During the summertime, hundreds of thousands of people walking around with solar panel caps, where they could plug in and charge their smartphones, right from their solar panel hats. The downfall of that would be thousands of people at a baseball game on a summer's day, wearing these solar panel caps. But instead of people watching the game, they are busy looking down at their phones. Since the batteries of their phones will never die on them, people would never get off of their phones. Batters would be hitting home runs, people would not even see the flyballs coming, and BAM! Oh my God, can you imagine that?

Never mind when I talked about eyelids, with these solar panel baseball caps, you will never see people's face ever again. People's heads would be bent down, engaged in their phones, the brim of the solar panel caps would completely cover their faces. I see it; clearly, people walking around with their smartphones plugged in their solar panel caps—the cord to their phones, connected to the hats, and those blue-lit screens. Then at nighttime, thousands of people walking around, looking like a bunch of Anglerfish. Oh, that would fit so perfectly too! Anglerfish are notorious for being angry and cranky, and how does social media make people feel? Exactly! Angry and cranky, just like an Anglerfish.

Everything is becoming smart now too. We have smartphones, smartwatches, smart T. V's, smart cars, smart rings, and even smart foods. Everything is smart now except us, human beings. How did it all come to this? We do not see each other as smart anymore unless we score high on a test. Spending years training students to excel on tests, but for the real test of life, we are failing the youth, crippling them, and preventing them from creating things that will inspire those to come. We rely on words to define us. Yes, that is how we communicate, of course. But what we feel on the inside, our actions and behavior is the real definition of our character. Words are tools that we use to express ourselves, to speak about how we feel. However, words can always be misleading and manipulating. We are so good at lying through our words. Telling people, "we are doing great," "living our best lives," "no worries." But the harsh reality is that we could be hurting, profoundly depressed, or trapped in our misery. But we do not see that on social media. Through social media, we have created an era of defining ourselves, defining our worth with words and numbers, and truth not being a priority. The truth has become too shallow for our interest and attention. Lies can dig deep, sinking our relationships and friendships.

I think about what the future will hold for our friendships and relationships, especially on social media sites. Will real friends, who are loyal to one another, last in this social media world that we are now living in right now? Do you have real friends? Hell, what are real friends? People come, and they go. Some stay for a long time, while others come around, and their presence is short-lived. I mentioned before; I believe that social media has disconnected and ruined more friendships and relationships than it has sustained or saved. Black and white friendships ruined by differences in political beliefs in this Trump era.

Having a friend; a friend who you spent time with, hung out with multiple times; all of a sudden unfollows you. You realize then that you were not as close as you once thought you were.

One of my mistakes was having my real friends and my family on social media. I have had experiences where I was unfollowed and blocked by friends and family. It makes things incredibly awkward when you see them in person. Having to pretend I did not know that I was unfollowed or blocked, and then seeing them later on. You may think it is not that important or serious, that a friend or family member removed you from social media. But I know it creates tension in real life, having that five-hundred-pound gorilla in the room.

I have this epiphany about real friends; and how social media has remedied that. Not only are real friends hard to come across in this social media world, but they are also rare to keep. I am probably the only one who feels that way, or at least I once did when I was logged on. But allow me to elaborate more on what I believe to be happening with friendships and relationships.

16 *Likes*

Real Friends

Not too long ago, I heard this song that was done by Hip Hop living legend; the teacher, Lawrence "Kris" Parker, also known as "KRS-One." KRS-One made a song called "*A Friend.*" The lyrics, the melodies, mixing the hip-hop flow with some orchestra, the piano, violin, and cello. The song tells a story of what a friend is. It is a sound that today's rappers are not expressing often. But of course, this is a different time we are now living in. So, you cannot expect the same sounds of the past, even though hip-hop during the nineties had a supreme quality, lyrically and musically.

That song makes me reflect on what a real friend is. So, I asked myself this question; "what are real friends?" Are real friends someone who just encourages you to follow your dreams; and motivates you daily? Are real friends, just people who help us in the severe stages that life puts us through? Are real friends, only people, or can they also be animals as pets? How do we know who our real friends are on social media?

When I was on these platforms; I met quite a few "friends," where we text back and forth for a reasonable amount of time; and then the next thing I know, they disappear. I looked them up on my friends' list; I noticed those friends, who I thought would be my ride or die; were nothing more but a slide and lie. They were a slide across the screen of my smartphone, to the direct messages, and just a bunch of lies that came with them.

Also, why? Just why do people come on your profile, follow you, and then not even a week later that same person unfollows you? Why is that? Did you not like enough of their post? Did you not show them enough attention? Did you miss out on "liking" one of their posts, and they felt some discomfort with your absence of their good news? How loyal can a real friend truly be, with social media being the untrustworthy bridge that keeps your friendship connected?

We have excessively trusted technology to keep our friendships and relationships connected. But how can you possibly expect to maintain a stable relationship with a partner, when you have hundreds, thousands, or millions of people in your business? Does that cause you any anxiety about your relationship, if you have one? I would bet you anything if you were to swap phones with your partner and explore what you have on each other's phones. By the time you get to each other's social media and direct messages, you both would have an anxiety attack or even break up.

That epiphany that I mentioned before about friendships and relationships on social media; here it is. Because of all this social media and technology, and the excessive use of it all. We have become a society of streaming. We are streaming music, streaming movies, television networks, podcast, and something else that I never thought could be possible. It dawned on me that people on social media are now streaming friendships and relationships.

Think about this; by following random strangers, sending and accepting "friend" request to people who you never even met before. You are streaming a friendship, subscribing to a bond that is not a real authentic friendship. When you hit that follow button on a person's profile, you get instant access to their success, love life, personal family affairs, careers, and everything else that they decide to share with their public following. On FB, it says friend request. So, you could be a "friend" with a person on FB for years and would never even meet them in person? You can like their photos, watch their videos, comment on their posts, and also wish them a happy birthday; but you have never met them in person, in real life? That, by definition, is streaming friendships and relationships. When you are no longer interested in this "friendship" or "relationship," you can willingly unfollow them. No loyalty required, whatsoever.

I will take it even further; we are potentially on the verge of streaming politics and politicians. To support my claim, go back and take a look at how Cambridge Analytica took millions of people's data from FB, bombarded people's news feeds with ads upon ads for Trump's presidential campaign. Then they manipulated the people into changing their behavior and eventually had them change who they voted for back in the 2016 presidential race. Streaming politicians, sending you ads, short commercials, calling out other politicians for their flaws. This has giving the masterminds behind the scenes, the opportunity to change your way of thinking; change who you vote for; allowing the machine to control you, and make you do anything it wants.

This is insane; that we have mistakenly created a world like this. A world where your thoughts are not your thoughts and your beliefs are not your beliefs. We are overly agreeing and disagreeing with each other. Social media has created the world's most prolonged debate in the history of humanity. Ever since FB started, it has created this worldwide debate that has been going on for the last fifteen years. A discussion with absolutely no compromise, a bunch of people just disagreeing and agreeing with each other online, and with no results whatsoever. People are just posting their lives away as if everyone on social media is a politician. I am sure that by now, almost every politician who is running for office, has some form of social media. Politicians are growing unprecedently into celebrities and superstars.

It is not even about what you do anymore; it is all a huge popularity game. Take Trump, for example; no political experience, just ran a bunch of businesses but never ran for any political offices. He just threw some slogans to the American people, some red hats, and then bam! He is now the 45th President of the United States of America, just like that. I hope that we never have a celebrity in the white house again. So far, we have two presidents who were elected during this social media era. We have a long way to go in this country when it comes to politics. God only knows what more chaos this next presidential election is going to cause. Along with the election after that, and the one after that. Streaming friendships, relationships, and politics. A world of producing false connections and beliefs; just because it is trending and fashionable to do so.

The thing about streaming friendships, when you are following people, you will keep seeing their profile over and over again. It will get to a point where you just become unbelievably tired of seeing their faces. It would not matter what new content people post; you will have had enough, and it would seem as if nothing has changed on their platform. So, you will then unfollow those people and put an end to those streaming friendships and relationships. You can delete them as a friend, unsubscribe, or block them without warning. Precisely what I said before about how people follow to unfollow you. The same way you can cancel a subscription with music and television networks; you can cancel a friendship with people on social media, and also in real life.

Think about this as well; if you are interested in someone but their profile is set to private, and then you send a follow request. You then have to wait anxiously to get that individual's final approval. But what happens if you are rejected? How would that make you feel? Would you, in your mind curse the person out? You would say the hell with them, right? That is the thing; social media has given us a whole new form of rejection. People are not letting you into their world, and rightfully so. Some of you do not want everyone in on your social media. You just prefer to have only family and real friends follow you, and that is entirely understandable.

But I am sure that the routine of only having loved ones follow you on social media never lasts long. You will eventually want to have some of those likes coming from random strangers and watch those numbers roll in. To be rejected on social media, that can destroy one's self-esteem. Making that person feel unworthy, or not good enough. The politics with this social media world is that people worship quantity over quality. People seem only to respect you based on the number of followers you have. If a person's profile does not have enough followers, they are not to be considered qualified or of importance. That is why these platforms are becoming more and more dangerous towards these kids. The kids believe the hype. These kids think they have to be on these sites, to have a growing following, to be accessible, and stay in the loop. Their young, fragile, naïve minds are being manipulated every single day they log on. What bothers me the most is how persuasive cyberbullying has become. Classmates and peers are teasing other kids online. I have seen multiple times, kids so engaged with their phones. Scrolling their thumbs up and down, wiping tears off the screen of their phones, weeping away at what cruelty they are enduring on social media.

Now, this is how disloyal people have become, in this social media world. Friendships and relationships are now a new form of streaming. People who are your friends online; it is impossible to stay in contact with everyone, of course. Think about what that can do to the relationships with your real friends in your actual real life. Now I am not saying that friendships are all fake on social media. There are people who have found their soulmates online, whether it was on social media, dating sites, Skype, etc. It is possible to find real friends and make real connections with these platforms. However, social media has a way of creating jealousy and speculations among your real friends. You ever had a moment when you went out to a party, post a picture, and one of your friends leaves a comment that said, "thanks for the invite," and you do not know what to say to them?

How about not making time for your close friends, you start to hang out with some new people, and you post pictures on Ivory with those new "friends." But the friends you are much closer to feels left out or abandon. Has that ever been your scenario? Yes, life is life; people move on and make new friends. We walk different paths and meet new people, and then to see all of this on social media, as a friend, it can, and it will take its toll.

Now some of you may read this and say that this epiphany, this whole streaming friendship, and relationship theory is not accurate. Maybe from your own experiences with friends on social media, this is not the case. That is fine, but I ask you to take some time and think about it. So that the next time you call someone a "friend" of yours, you can use this analogy and apply it to whoever you cross paths with, in the future. Real friends are somewhat challenging to hold onto in the world we live in today. It may not seem this way because people post photos with their friends and show the good times, but we do not see the truth; the whole truth. The narratives of people's posts can be so manipulative and so far from the truth on social media.

As of right now, the real friends that I have are very few but are very real. I stay in contact and see them from time to time. I must say that the conversations are very genuine and also natural. My friends are on social media, but since I am not, I interact with my friends via phone call, text, or just an uncomplicated rendezvous somewhere to catch up on things. My absence from social media benefits me by not ruining the moments that I share with my friends. They can personally inform me of their updates on new jobs, personal matters, new relationships, having kids, and many other things.

Everything that my friends share with me would be surprising news to me.

I have been able to be a better friend to them because of my absence. I can be more attentive to what they are saying and not be distracted by my phone. I am in the moment with my friends, I listen to what they have to say, and that is a beautiful thing. I love having real friends without the need of a third party getting involved in our bond. My dream for the future is to have a partner who is on the same wavelength as me. To have a beautiful, healthy relationship, where she has also taken a permanent self-dismissal from social media, so that we can have an actual, real private life together, with no external interference. Just the two of us. But the way things are going on, in this era of posts, likes, and views, I fear that to be more of a pipe dream. To find true love and to keep true love without the surveillance of social media and technology.

I mentioned before how time is a disease that we want to have forever. But now I want to go deeper into how we as people have been using time since the very beginning. We use time as a direction.

17 *Likes*

Time Is Our Compass

Time is not what we believe it to be. We look at our watches and think that is real-time, when, in actuality, that is just a compass. The time that we see on our watches, smartwatches, alarm clocks, smartphones, and clocks all over the world; are only numbers that control and guide our everyday lives. It is the compass that we use daily that tells us when it is time to get up and get ready for work. It tells us when we have to show up for work, the time of breakfast, lunch and dinner, and it tells us when we are late. Time even lets us know how long we have been living on this earth, and every time we made it to a new year.

I believe that time, in a way, is artificial intelligence. There is no possible way for us human beings to be able to know how old exactly our planet is, or the universe itself. So, how can we possibly believe that the time we use today is accurate to the earth when the earth is approximately billions of years old? Human beings have only been in existence for the last several hundred thousand years. I understand that religion and astrology play a massive part in how we identify time today.

However, I really do stand by "time" being a compass to our lives, guiding us throughout all the different walks of life. I look at it now; I understand a lot more why holidays are so important. Holidays, birthdays, and anniversaries are checkpoints. They let us know how far ahead in time we went through in life, and how much time we have left to prepare for the next holiday. Most importantly, time is used so that we do not forget or become lost on this planet. When you look at it, time is an enormous privilege that we have on this earth. Time is like money, yes, but if I could help it, I would always prefer to have more time on this earth, than to have money.

You can lose money one day, and the next day hit the lottery for millions of dollars. But if you waste time, even five minutes of it, that is something you can never get back. We can turn back clocks and watches all we want, but that will never give us those five minutes back. There is no guarantee on how much time we get on this earth. Time is truly a numbers game that we play in this life. Like right now, as I am writing, I took a quick glimpse at the time on my television. The time says 7:23 p.m. I find it amazing how much numbers do control us and our minds. The figures in our bank accounts, our credit scores, SAT scores, and now, the numbers on social media. Even the numbers on a weight scale can manipulate our self-esteem and our insecurities. Numbers are everywhere, along with time. That is why I said time is a compass. It gives us directions for our walks of life.

Time is also frustrating when it comes to our jobs. For example, an employee could be running ten minutes late to work, and their supervisor is looking at their watch. As the employee arrives ten minutes late, the supervisor now sees that employee as irresponsible. The supervisor is now looking at this employee with a disappointing face. That is what time has turned us into, into these judgmental people. Also, time deals with our physical growth. You know that saying, "where has the time gone?" People say that when they see their children grow up and they just cannot believe that time goes by so rapidly.

Now I know after reading this, you are probably thinking to yourself, "what does time have to do with social media?" Well, I do not know how much time you spend on social media. Still, I have a feeling that some people who will read this book spend well more than two hours a day, not just on their phones, but two hours a day on social media alone. Two hours of scrolling up and down a screen, looking at other peoples' lives. As I said before, we dedicate so much of our precious time on social media, time that we will never get back, and for what? For "likes"? Giving other people "likes"?

Twelve years was too much time spent on platforms that did not give me direction. It did not help me by dedicating so much of my time, only to get in return, some instant validation and numbers that were not relevant. I had put a value on my existence based off of those numbers. I thought that was my success, but it was indeed my failure. I just do not wish failure on any of you. Our time on this earth is all we have to offer one another. I do believe that is one of our purposes in life; to share our time. To share our time with our families, our friends, loved ones, even our pets, and of course, reserving some time for ourselves. For us to share our time, so much of our time to these tech god gadgets, we have broken the bonds that we once considered important. I understand what social media has been ideally designed to do; to connect people for social networking. But who can manage their time to entertain hundreds, thousands, millions of followers? No human being on this earth has the time to stay in contact with but so many people. So why, why spend so much time on these social media platforms, so much time on these devices? Some may say that social media money is good. The thing about money is you have to give it right back to your bills, your food, your public appearances, your wardrobe, and your management team. That alone is another game you must play.

I kid you not; I would instead go hiking in the woods for two hours a day than to spend two hours on social media, watching other people go hiking and liking their post. I would rather spend two hours working out in the gym than scrolling up and down, watching other people getting in shape, watching the social media yoga and fitness instructors, the social media influencers, the celebrities, and then comparing your life to theirs. I will repeat this; there may come a time when these machines will stop. If these machines were to crash, and all of your sharing of your life will vanish. Can you imagine what this would do to people? Especially young people? All of your family photos, pictures of your newborn babies, weddings, anniversaries, all of your precious memories, to disappear. I will tell you this; never put the trust of holding on to sacred moments, friendships, relationships, into an app on your phone.

How do you expect these current platforms to last forever? The innovators of the future will just keep creating new social media sites; that will keep sucking the life and time out of you. As I said earlier, we, as human beings, have become the batteries that keep these apps running. We are, in a way, the humanized energizer bunnies. We are using our irreversible time and energy to give these machines life. One day you will look down at your phone, and by the time you look back up, a whole decade will have gone by so swiftly. That is what it felt like for me. I wish I could have that time again; I sincerely do. It would be one thing if I did some things in life that I would consider a failure. But for me to be so committed to social media for years, wasting my time, I have failed enough.

I just pray that you who are reading this; you give yourself a chance to reevaluate yourself. I pray that you try to reserve some of your time and protect it from these seductive platforms. Once again, I do not know you, and I do not want to assume anything. I do not know how much time you spend on social media or how active you are daily. But I just do not wish any burdens on you. I do not want you to fall into the excessive use of this stuff and solely rely on these platforms to be your meal ticket to a better life. Go for a better life experience of just having real friends. People who love you and not people who are just "liking" you and your posts.

Now is the time. We are now in the twentieth year of the twenty-first century, if that is the accurate time we are living in, right? By the time this book is in your hands, and you are reading it; we will be finishing up the first quarter of 2020; the beginning of a new decade. Unless, of course, those who may be reading this one day, who are living in the year 2055; hello to you, thirty-five years in the future.

But yes, the year 2020. A new decade that could be the change you make for yourself. A move that you genuinely need to make. Now is the time to stop defining yourself with numbers and establish yourself with character, ethics, integrity, your spirit, and with the truth.

Get your time back! When you get your time again, you get your life back. By all means, take your time to think about all of this. Think about how much this could help you in the long run. How beneficial taking a break from these platforms could be. If you even decide to quit all of the social media and escape, as I said before, you have my full support. You have my full support and trust me when I tell you; you will not miss out on any opportunities that bring real value to your life. For your actual value is the time you have on this earth and what you make of it. If you decide to stay on social media, but reduce your time of using it, I can respect that and understand. You do not need my approval or anyone's approval for that matter. Some of you may have endorsements deals or some business obligations that keep you in the social media loop; I get it. No judgments at all; reducing your time on social media, that is a brilliant start. If some of you decide to remove yourselves from social media entirely, once again, whoever you are, wherever you are, you have made a courageous choice. You have my full support, and most importantly, you are not alone.

I have this other theory about time. I have this theory about three things; the wealthy, jobs, and time theory: you may not understand where I am coming from, or maybe some of you will. But I will just say this—the wealthy, wealthy people who have endless amounts of money, billions upon billions of dollars. So much money, that money is no longer money to them; money is now their product. Now stay with me on this theory. Money for the wealthy is the real product they must sell to some of the public. But how does one sell money? Well, they market their product (money) with jobs, for a selective group of people, who they call employees; who can do those jobs exceptionally well. The wealthy gives these employees a job to do, but you see the thing is; the occupation is the necessary middleman. The real exchange is merely between the rich and the poor. The wealthy person sells the money, and the employee pays for it, with their precious time, out of their dear life. Employees' valuable "time," something they can never get back, is what employees use to buy the "money" product from wealthy people. I am not talking about tangible products, such as a phone, but the "money" product from the wealthy. Employees buy wealthy people's money with their time. Think about it; the U.S. treasury creates the money; the wealthy people along with their investors and teams create the jobs; then a selective group of people are hired for those jobs, which requires those people to dedicate their time, their valuable time, out of their lives, in exchange for those paychecks from the wealthy people.

Jobs are these made up entities that could disappear at any given moment. If a corporation were to downsize or go bankrupt, it would be as if the jobs never existed. There is a thin line between the rich and the poor; that thin line is jobs. Jobs the wealthy creates and offers to the poor. Jobs the poor accepts and spend years of their lives slaving away their time, and that is what pays for the money. When I say poor, of course, I am speaking from an economic standpoint, not from a person's weak character, or poor behavior. That is why when I hear of people who have been working the same job for decades. People who paid for money with so much time out of their lives. I understand that and say, "You must respect the working class of America." People have sacrificed half of their lives, only to purchase the real ultimate product, money. We all are an employee to someone, even if you are your own boss. Now I understand why some employees always want a raise in their jobs. They feel that their time is worth so much more than the minimum wage that the wealthy sells to them. They are very right. Jobs have been created simply to cut the greed so they can bleed a little of that money out.

That is the game we live in, this money game. Time is like money now, right? Sounds crazy to some, I bet. That is because it is a bit bizarre. What did I say earlier? We are the only living species on this planet that has to worry about money, taxes, and bills. We have to worry about countries, states, cities, governments, religions, and who owns the land. No other mammals or animals have to worry about these things. No one can ask a lion, a tiger, or a horse, "what do you want to be when you grow up?" Animals cannot talk, so you would not get an answer to that question. But the answer to that is nothing. Animals will grow up to be what they were born to be. It is only us people who have to work our whole lives. Now maybe some of you will understand why we as humans feel so isolated and lonely on this earth. We are the only ones who have to make a living, rather than just living. Just living life and enjoying life to the fullest, enjoying our existence. But no, we have to pay for all of that, with our time, in exchange for money. We have isolated ourselves from all the other living species; to feel unique and superior.

Now, of course, with all of that being said; this is what we have to do, period! We have to work; we have to take care of ourselves and our families. What I wanted you to get from this theory, whether you are young or old. What you choose to do in this life, just make sure you love what you do. That way, when you are working, paying for that money with your precious time, you do not ever get what is called "buyer's remorse."

18 *Likes*

Celebrities on Social Media

Celebrities, the rich, and the world-famous. The red carpets; lights, cameras, SOCIAL MEDIA! Stars on social media. They have it the worst; addiction I mean. As if they needed a platform to showcase their lavish, luxurious, one-percenter lifestyles to the masses. They are showing their foreign cars, jewelry, window shopping clothes, flaunting the "good life," right in the world's faces.

I said this earlier, I do not acknowledge them as celebrities or stars anymore. I can no longer put celebs on the pedestal of a supreme perception. Do you know how I see them now? I see them only as people. Do you know who helped me observe them merely as people? Kanye West. As I said earlier, I have Kanye West to thank for changing my perception of "celebrities."

Kanye West, to me, is an unsung hero. Now before you think in your mind and say, "WHAT?!!" I know some of you may be thinking, "how in the hell is Kanye West a hero?" Allow me to elaborate on that. When Kanye went on TMZ, ranting for about ten minutes, talking about how he was on certain medications, and making his comments about how "slavery was a choice." When I heard Kanye say what he said about slavery, Kanye broke something in me; he broke this spell that I was under for so many years. A spell of me believing in what celebrities have to say. In what celebrities have to say every time they get on stage to accept an award and then have this speech about what we need to do as a people. Celebrities are saying, "we have to do this and do that." The things stars say or do in interviews; are all just for entertainment. After Kanye ranted on TMZ, he showed me that celebrities do not have all the answers. They do not have any answers; at least not any that helps the general public. All these years, all these celebrities, yet kids are still dying; drugs are still being used, alcohol, just no real changes are being made. But I must say that Kanye West has changed me forever after that moment of his meltdown.

Kanye showed me that even celebrities, athletes, and entertainers could be off the path at times. The famous can be wrong and out of line; the rich and powerful can be ignorant and uneducated. When all the glitz and glamor go away, celebrities are nothing more, but human beings, just like me. I mean yes, celebrities can make some great music, they can act, shoot some three-pointers, score some touchdowns, and what have you. But when it comes to uplifting the world, only very few have been able to do that. So, from that point on, I realized I did not have to feel nervous or insecure around rich and famous people ever again. I could just be myself. I no longer have to feel the need to walk up to a celebrity and ask for a picture. Kanye basically helped aligned my perception with reality, the way it should be; I believe that.

Now, does Kanye West have some personal problems? I do not know him. I never met him before, so I do not want to pass judgment on him. However, I just feel Kanye loves those cameras and microphones. When he is in front of them, he performs with endless amounts of energy and the everlasting release of dopamine. See for yourself; almost every time Ye gets in front of cameras and microphones; it is like he cannot control himself. It is like cake and ice cream for him. I wonder who Kanye is when there are no cameras or microphones around him.

I want to touch on something else about Kanye, and about reality. When you stop to think about what Kanye's journey has been. His life in and out of the music business. I think of this man and his relationship with reality. I feel that Kanye, in his mind, feels so betrayed by reality. Think about it; he was involved in a car accident that almost took his life; he lost his best friend, his momma, so suddenly. Perhaps Kanye just thought one day, "the hell with reality, I'm just going to live in fantasyland, where anything is possible; live in fantasy until reality takes me out." So, every time when Kanye goes on a rant, in a way, I believe that is just a big "F*%# you" to reality. That is the only way he can find his healing; that and his devotion to God. I believe we can all relate to that feeling of being betrayed by reality. I remember watching Kanye in an interview with Charlamagne Tha God, A.K.A "Uncle Charla."

Kanye talked about how Trump inspired him to run for president. Kanye believed after Trump was assigned as president, that anything is possible. Here is the thing; I do believe that anything is possible. However, possibility without purpose or integrity is nothing more but possibility without satisfaction. If you have no real meaning, moral value, or purpose in why you want to achieve something in life, it will just leave you empty on the inside after you have achieved it, and that will then leave you to be impossible to deal with, period! That is what the world of social media has done. People have made the impossible, possible; yet achieving the impossible generated no satisfaction, posting things that go viral, and then after that fades away, people lose themselves, and trying to find yourself on social media, is without a doubt; impossible. Trump did the impossible. He made it possible, with no integrity, no morals, and now he is impossible to deal with. After he was acquitted of impeachment, no one can tell him nothing now.

Now, as far as reality. Reality is sometimes excruciating for all of us. We lose our loved ones so suddenly, with no explanation, no warning, nothing at all; they are gone forever. It leaves us in shock, devastated, and we just cannot believe it. That is another reason why social media is so inconvenient at times. Family members who hear about loved ones dying via social media, before having it confirmed by someone in the immediate family. Then all the postings and hashtags, "#RIP, #Restinpeace, #gonebutnotforgotten." These tech tears are just weird to me. People are just burying their loved ones in this digital dirt of social media, the computer bugs and worms we call algorithms just eats at them. Our loved ones will never be able to rest on these platforms. I made the mistakes of taking someone's death, and reducing it to a post, just for "likes."

Another thing about social media is this; we have been so programmed by this world, this world of make-believe, that when reality hits us, we just cannot accept it at all! Reality does not resonate with us as quickly anymore. My take on reality and losing a loved one is this; I deal with reality the best way I can. I deal with reality with two key elements: love and appreciation—my love for the people in my life, living or deceased—also, the appreciation of having a life and the people who are in it. When I had to face the reality that my grandfather was dying, I faced it head-on and decided to take care of him in his last days. I will say this; we had some good days, and we had some bad days. But I appreciate the fact that I was there for all of it. Because when I was there for him, I gained some of the greatest memories of him and my grandmother. They were there for each other until the very end. I will remember those moments forever, and I know they are okay, they are reunited, and I will forever have them in my heart until we meet again. In reality, the pain will always be there, but so will the love. The pain will win some battles, but love will always win the war. Do not ever forget that.

But I do mean what I say though; Kanye West forever changed how I feel about the whole "celebrity" atmosphere. It would not matter if public figures such as Michael Jordan, Paul McCartney, even the Pope, or whoever of that level of fame. If they were to pass me or also to meet them, I would be calm and collective. I would not ask for pictures or autographs. I would just introduce myself, say hello, and keep it moving.

Everything that I once believed about celebrities changed for me when Kanye said what he said on TMZ. I changed for the better because of him, and I thank him for that. I guess sometimes it takes a broken person to break cycles that are happening in other people's lives. It was disturbing how people responded to this brother about what he said. I know Kanye said some foul, incorrect, negative, hurtful things in the media, and he has his problems with collogues in the music and fashion industry. But I am sure he means well. However, it is hard sometimes for one to mean well when he or she is not well. Kanye West is a human being, just like me, and just like you. What I admire about him is his fearlessness to be wrong, but I just wish he did not make such a cruel statement. The slavery remark was cruel, soulless, and heartless. I hope I never hear another black man speak that out loud again, or even have that on his mind. What did I say before? Do not say or do the "wrong" things, just because you have the "right" to do them.

Celebrity; is not what it once was. It is not the same; after Michael Jackson and Prince left this earth, I felt that we lost some of the last world stoppers. What I mean by world stoppers; the world practically stopped when we lost them. These days, celebrities have no mystery whatsoever. You know why? Because just about all of them are on social media. They are all posting their lives away, just as addicted as anyone else, I believe. They are posting pictures of their kids, their kids' names and nicknames, their pets, their whole families. Then when their fans approach them, and the fans know the names of all their family members, I bet celebrities wonder how their fans know so much. Because celebrities post too much, way too much information. Also, they know where celebs live, what hotels they are staying at; stars have made themselves way too accessible because of these social media platforms.

You cannot tell me that celebrities do not get excited when they see all those likes, those comments, and new followers exploding every time they post a viral bound selfie or a sexy half-nude pose. How about their verified blue check? When they feel like somebody on those platforms.

I do not believe celebrities understand something when it comes to social media. After I quit social media; I heard at times when I was on set talking with other actors; they would say to me, "You need it! You need social media!" As I said before, likes on a post or a few new followers are not going to make me a better actor. These platforms are designed to keep you addicted. But yes, people would tell me that I need social media and celebrities; they just love it.

There are a few things that I believe celebrities may not have thought of before. Most of the stars who are in their forties and up, they come from an older generation, another time, a different world. A time where smartphones and social media were not even an echo of a whisper in a person's ear. Older celebs had a life way before these gadgets and platforms came into fruition. They do not realize that a lot of these kids were born in this social media world. My point is this; if or when these platforms crash, for an extended period, some of these celebrities will not be hurting. They will still have their money, their lifestyle, their careers, and their fame. The younger generation of people, who do not have much, it will be as if they have lost their whole identity, their entire lives. So, for anyone who says you need social media, it is like telling someone they need a distraction. They need to have an addiction.

Also, older celebrities have to realize; they were well established before social media existed. Most of the stars had millions of fans behind them; so, coming on to social media to build their brand was technically a breeze. But even with a celebrity's profile, they come across the bots and avatar profiles. I do not think celebs realized that when they retaliate with those profiles that leave negative comments on their pages, those are the bots and avatars, not real people.

It is unfortunate; to even hear how some celebrities who opened up a social media account, they purchased packages of fake followers to create the illusion of being relevant, using numbers to feel special. What in God's name? Why? Why are these platforms so crucial to our lives now? Why is it so important for the rich and famous? Every time I would see these interviews with celebs, and see their social media profiles under their names, it just reminds me of what I said about people one day having their profile names on their tombstone.

Social media has evolved celebrities into a digital meritocracy. Having celebs posting ads for these random companies; that does not even fit their character or their brand. I remember seeing a famous comedian on social media, who posted an ad for a toll-free number for student loan forgiveness. When I saw that, that was the starting point of breaking that celebrity spell. To see famous women making videos for fat burning shakes. I asked myself, "are people even fans to celebrities anymore, or are they just consumers?" It is not living; this is simply not living.

I had some interesting experiences with celebrities on set before. Some were great experiences; others were not so great. There was this one time that I worked on a television show, and I was working with this one actor, who I will keep anonymous. This experience with this particular actor pretty much had hit the nail in the coffin for me, as far as not seeing celebrities as celebrities anymore. Kanye sparked it for me, but this actor sealed the deal. It was the last day of shooting; the last shot of the final scene, the martini shot, is what they call it. So, as I stood there on set, the director yells, "cut, check the gate, and that is a wrap." The actor then makes his way towards me, reaches out to shake my hand, and as he shakes my hand, he sarcastically says, "I hope you learned something." As if watching him act, I was supposed to watch and learn; to be good just like him. You see, I was a stand-in at that time. My job was to be the stand-in for the principal actors and rehearse scenes for the lighting and camera crew. I was standing-in for that actor. But that came as no surprise, because the way he carried himself so arrogantly on set, it was a matter of time before that energy would be coming towards me. The egos of some people are just beyond me; they cannot help themselves.

That is the thing about egos. I believe that our egos come from two sources: our problems and our insecurities. Our issues and insecurities are like miners. They dig their way deep into our souls, our minds, and they just stay there. They dig in so deep inside of us, to find the gems within—our gems of happiness, love, ideas, and truth. Then when our issues and insecurities find those gems inside of us, they turn them into jewelry, which then becomes our egos. They take our happiness, our love, ideas, and truth; and reduce them to these fragile egos. Now you may understand why some of the rich and famous have the biggest egos. Their egos hide their problems and insecurities. But after a while, the jewelry will begin to devalue. Their happiness will turn into sadness, love into hate, ideas into spam thoughts, and truth into lies.

That is why so many of these celebrities out there are just losing their minds; overdosing on drugs, alcoholism, and it only gets worse. Because now these famous people have large followings on social media, judging them every step of the way. Then these celebs go on a live video, at the peak of their vulnerability, speaking their business, ranting about things that are not for the world to know about, just for the attention.

I believe that is what happened to Kanye West, to Donald Trump, to that arrogant actor I was a standing-in for, that is also what happened to that casting director, who I mentioned before. These celebrities are programmed the most on these platforms. The tragedy is most of them do not even know it. It is so disturbing to hear celebrities brag about how many followers that got, how many likes they get on a post, or how their last video went viral with millions of views. The day I saw reverend Al Sharpton post a selfie in front of a mirror, looking like Kat Williams, I said to myself, "the black movement is just about over." I mean, of course, some of you are probably saying, "let the man live!" But still, everyone and their grandparents are on social media, infatuated with those “likes.”

Seeing celebs go on a live video, going back and forth, beefing with other celebrities, them looking down at their phones, watching the comments shoot up, along with the emojis. I remember seeing those live videos; looking in those celebrities' eyes; I would just see nothing on the inside. No, that is not true; I did see somethings in their eyes while I was looking at their live videos; back when I was on social media, of course. I saw a lot of desperation and validation seeking. The vulnerability, the fear, the depression, confusion, most importantly, I saw myself in them. I saw everything that I was becoming within them. The only difference is, I did not have the fortune or fame to hide the pain; the same pain that I saw in all those celebrities' eyes, I saw in myself when I looked in the mirror. I could not hide my pain any longer with selfies on set, or selfies with celebrities. I became so sick and tired of it all. I just did not want to be that man, that man who says, "I posted this the other day, and it got so many likes."

Between smartphones and social media, they destroyed everything about "being in the moment." Could you imagine, smartphones and social media being around during the sixties? Imagine a bunch of kids recording Jimi Hendrix setting his guitar on fire, and not truly being in the moment of that experience. People who were there at the Monterey Pop Festival, back in 1967, to this day, are still talking about what they experienced, with the Jimi Hendrix Experience. Nothing like that has ever happened before that time, nothing like that has happened ever since. Even if it did, people would just waste that moment away by recording and posting it to social media, just for likes and views.

To the celebrities, I know you have a lot of money and fame. But as long as you have all these platforms, there is one thing you will never have, ever again, and that is privacy! With your lifestyle and your highly demanding careers, privacy is your sanity, your therapy even. Trust me, I said this before, and this certainly can apply to you as well; you owe no one a post or video of your success. I do not know who died and said we need social media to be a success, but whoever that person was, that person died for nothing.

Of course, as I say once again, I am not telling you what to do with your life. Have a ball with your social media accounts, if that is what you choose to do. Post get your likes, your comments, your views, and your followers. But if I may say one thing, keep some kind of mystery. Try to reserve at least seventy-five percent of your life and who you are to yourselves. Why do you think Michael Jackson and Prince were who they were? Because they kept some mystery about themselves and who they were personally. They did not do too many interviews; they did not just put themselves all out there on the table. The mystery about them is what made and kept them magical.

Then again, who am I to say. For some of the celebrities, social media is what made them famous. It made them who they are today. But that is what I fear for the younger generations to come, who will be relying solely on these apps to make them feel worthy and enough. They will do whatever it takes to be famous, yet do nothing at all to be smart and educated. Prime example; rapper "6ix9ine" and actor "Jussie Smollett." Look at what they did for fame and attention, which then turned infamous. Look at how far people will go for these social media platforms. I know the feds, C.I.A, and law enforcement are having a field day, catching criminals via social media.

There is something odd about the rap genre today. I feel that rap has become a foster parent; that is producing a generation of juvenile delinquents and rejects. Everyone is pushing to be a rapper. Pretty soon, the mumble rappers will turn into humming rappers, and then there will be deaf rappers, rapping in sign language. Then after that, rap will just be a bunch of kids in music videos, high as all hell, dancing to the beats like zombies; no lyrics required. Millions of other zombies will worship those new zombie rappers. Not saying that some of these rappers are not talented, but as I said before, talent will be a thing in the past, and success will only be based on likes, views, and followers. Unless there are some behavioral changes made in this world or if people take a conscious step away from social media.

I know for some of you; as you are reading this chapter, you are probably trying to process this whole "celebrity" topic. To summarize it, Kanye West changed my life for the better by showing me that even he himself can make some foul choices or say some horrific things that are irreversible. Kanye humanized celebrities for me and showed me that from the riches, most famous of them all, they are just people; human beings who do not have all the answers in this life.

Now, of course, I am not telling you, the reader, that if you see your favorite celebrity, not to ask for an autograph or picture. By all means, have your moment with them; you most definitely do not need any approvals from me. I am not saying that these athletes, singers, dancers, actors, whoever you consider to be famous, are not influential to you. I am not saying that I no longer care about famous people. I will always love their music, their movies, their artwork, what they do for sports; I am fully aware that they are a hero to millions, all over the world.

However, I have changed my perception of how I see celebrities. No matter how great they are at what they do, I can now just see them for who they are. I see them as flesh and blood, human beings, with lives to live—families of their own to take care of, children to raise, just like anyone else. I will never see them as people who have all the answers to life, but more so as people who are searching for answers, just as you or myself would. It has been more liberating for me ever since.

What I hope you will get out of this particular chapter is never to try to compare your lives with the lives of the rich and famous. Because at the end of the day, celebrities are just seen as numbers. By numbers, I mean, their popularity, their talents, their looks, are all number generators. They bring in the revenue for the big-time corporations, and that is all those corporations see in celebrities; they see dollar signs.

Also, I am not saying that all celebrities are these egotistical, rude, arrogant individuals who think they can walk on water. I met some incredible people in that celebrity world, who I respect very much so. It is just from now on; I will rely on my experiences and memories with "celebrities." I will not always need a photo every time I come across them. To be honest with you, I do not even look at the pictures I took with celebrities from before. Those pictures are long gone; on my old smartphones. That is what I meant earlier, about when I said how I would take selfies with celebrities, using their fame as a coupon, for more likes, comments, and followers. Those days are over now; for me, at least.

Here in America, celebrities are everything to us. The musicians, the actors, artists, fashion designers, and of course, politicians. They are worshipped, loved, followed everywhere they go. Since America has no royal families, celebrities are all we have to brag about to the world. Because of that, stars pay the ultimate price…no privacy.

The compelling force to address their business on social media. Celebrities finding out their love partner was cheating on them, initially finding out via the internet. Then they have to isolate themselves from social media and deactivate their platforms. The "post and deletes," the constant "watch what you say and what you post" paranoia on a daily basis—celebrities are tweeting things and receiving thousands of comments, and all the backlashes. The insincere apologies, making donations to charities to make up for their irresponsible posts or statements.

Some celebrities, or should I say popular social media influencers, are under such an illusion that their voice is so powerful; in some cases, they are. But a powerful voice that is strategically blinded by numbers; eventually, their voice will just be screaming for help. Celebrities cannot see the truth; they cannot see what damage it has done while they are still logged on; no one can. No one who is on these platforms can peep the game.

But I am here; I logged off; I gave it all up. I had my self-intervention for my addiction to social media. Let this book be an intervention for you; the celebrities, in fact, everyone. Let go; put these phones down for a while and pick your heads back up. We are now living in this "heads down, likes up" society. Everyone is looking down now, looking down at these phones. Celebs are constantly tweeting and posting the craziest topics, personal business, new ideas, and random thoughts.

That was my problem now that I think about it. Every time I had an idea, I could not wait to post or tweet about it. I did not even let it marinate in my mind long enough to give myself peace of mind, to provide myself with some encouragement or self-support. I was more concerned with helping others with my words on social media, that I did not reserve those ideas and thoughts to make myself a better person. I became empty-minded. Now I understand why I was so quiet for so many years; all that I had to say, I posted it on social media, for likes. I simply posted; who I, Jordan Wells, was, but I did not live as Jordan Wells; if that makes any sense. My mentality at that time, who I was as a person in real life, was not half as important as who I projected myself to be on social media. I did not care much about my reality; social media was my only reality. Except it was not reality at all.

Now do you understand how screwed up I was, because I did not take a break from these platforms? Once again, I am not saying that this will happen to you, whether or not you are a celebrity, influencer, or whoever. I just had to give you at least a sincere warning. I had to tell you that if you do not take a break from any of these platforms, the possibilities of addiction will be waiting for you. Chances are, the habit is already there with you. The addiction is there, especially if your phone is in bed with you like it is the new electronic teddy bear. It is there when you check it first thing in the morning, it is there even when you do not have your phone on you, it is there, in your mind, in your consciousness.

Trust me when I tell you this; I had a problem. I seriously do not want you to have the same issues I endured from the misuse of these platforms. My life was heading towards a never-ending, downward spiral, that I could not climb my way out of for dear life. The constant checking of my phone, the noises, the notifications, vibrations, and many shedding tears that were from not liking what I saw, scrolling up and down those news feeds.

I just also think about whenever the world loses a celebrity, how people all of a sudden post dozens of pictures. I guess in the way of paying their respects to that celebrity and their family. To this day, I still do not know how to feel about that. It is like seeing thousands of obituaries all over social media. People buy as much memorabilia as they can as soon as that celebrity passes away. The "RIP" hashtags, yet those likes are still there. The same thing, over and over, "no words," "my condolences," "this can't be true." Forgive me for saying, but I can never, and will never shed these digital tears ever again. I am sure when people post their condolences, that they are sincere. But I just never trusted them with that “like” button associated with the post.

The other thing is, as I said before, you just never know if the rest of the family even heard anything. The last thing you ever want to find out via social media is your loved one has passed away before finding out from the family. That must be the worst experience ever, especially of someone famous.

I do not know if a celebrity will ever come across reading this book. Take it from me; the rain is not worth the cloud. Your career will not be in danger if you choose to let go of this lifestyle of likes, views, followers, and false validation. You will be better than ever. By letting go, not only will you be the star that people love so dearly, you will be human again. You will have your space; you will have your peace, your serenity, and your salvation, even as a celebrity. You will gain some privacy back into your life. Give it a try; let these platforms go. Let it be history and keep the mystery.

19 *Likes*

Keep the Mystery

Who I am as a person, as a man, a human being, will always be a work in progress. I do not believe you can ever know someone completely. There will always be something that you never noticed or discovered about people who you know personally. What I did on social media was I disclosed so much of who I was, who I thought I was, and who I wanted to become. What I did not realize back then is that I was not keeping any mystery about myself. I just wanted to be an open book; let everyone know my plans, my goals, my dreams, just almost everything about me. I did that so much; that I did not even know who I was anymore. I put so much information about myself online that there was nothing left inside of me mentally or spiritually to discover. All of my ideas and thoughts, my quotes, I would just share them on social media. No creativity left to reserve for me.

It felt as if I lost myself to my own free will. I lost hope and faith in myself as a person, a better person precisely. I did not keep any mystery for myself, and I was helpless. The worst feeling to have is not knowing yourself. I was so far away from happiness; I was far away from success. I was the farthest away, from me. When I was on social media, I did not hate or love myself. I could not feel either way because I did not know who I was anymore. Anything that was about me or that happened to me, I posted it all to my social media accounts. Even when I went to the hospital, I posted a picture of myself lying in the hospital bed. I exchanged information on my personal life for some numbers; likes, views, followers, and comments from random strangers with random opinions.

I gave these platforms years that I can never get back. All of the achievements that I forgot about because I was so quick to post and get the approval of random strangers. I cared more about the acceptance and validation from other people and their opinions. I did not take the time to enjoy the achievements on my own. I had arguments with people on social media. I was reading and delivering negative comments to people, trying to prove an irrelevant point. Letting people get under my skin and not thinking about the consequences to come from interacting with those strangers, and sometimes with people I knew or met in real life.

It took me such a long time to stop and say to myself, "this is not me; this is not Jordan Wells." Had I not escaped this social media world; I would have become something that I would never have ever imagined myself to be. I would have become the worst asshole to everyone. I would have become a negative, regressive person, a person of no faith, no passion, no ambition, and no dreams at all. All of this would have happened; just because I did not want to miss out on anything. I did not want to let go of my addiction. I tried to hold on to the drama and lies that social media is excellent for feeding us. I simply was not happy, not mentally healthy, and not sure of who the hell I was.

There was no mystery about me whatsoever. I wanted people to be up to date on everything. I would even say I became predictable. I would post, post, and post some more. I did not even care how many likes I would get. I just gave it all up for the attention. Just to see who would show up and show me "love." It came to the point where I would just post a selfie on SC, just to fill a views quota, as if it was an attendance sheet, making sure I had consistent viewers. It was a sickness that I had. It is tough to speak about all of this; because I would never have thought I could reduce myself to this low-life level. To hit rock bottom, from apps on my phone. I guess that would be the same thoughts that go through the mind of alcoholics, food, or drug addicts. They would not think that these things would get to them and destroy who they once were.

But there will always be light at the end of the tunnel. I logged off; I escaped each one of those platforms that caused me a great distraction, which then turned into depression and self-destruction. Some who may have met me or followed me on social media, who will read this, may say that they had no idea that I was going through all of this. Well, that is the gag; social media is not meant for us to see the truth behind our posts. I was faking the funk for a very long time. From the looks of it, people may have thought that I was happy from my post; but happiness was just as much of a stranger to me as the random strangers on social media. I was not at all a happy person. I was lying; lying for likes. I lied to manipulate people's perception of me. Now, I am not saying that I am a terrible person in real life. I am genuinely the opposite. I just made myself look so perfect on social media. I even had moments where I would get a little cocky and post shirtless photos. When I look back at that now, I just say "Wow!" I was not in my real character.

I should have never stayed on social media for so long, without a break. What I learned is that the longer you do something without a break; eventually, it will break you. Social media broke me down; I had to mold myself back together and be better than the person I was before. I cannot go back on those things; as I said, the addiction would just be waiting for me. I let those platforms get the best of me for those twelve years.

That is what I would suggest to those of you who will decide to continue on your social media journey. If you continue to use these platforms, make sure you keep some mystery about yourself. As I said before, you are not obligated, nor do you owe people a post into your lives. If you do not have anything to say or post, do not even bother that day. You do not have to relate to irrelevant things. I am sure some people have cut classes or skip school at some point in their lives. Try to treat social media with that same energy. Skip a few days of checking your social media. Again, I am not trying to tell you what to do, unless if you are looking for that answer. My answer would simply be not to use these platforms anymore. It is that simple for me. When I escaped the social media world, I was making that my final answer, a final decision. I am just really looking so forward to life without social media. It has already been over a year now for me, but just thinking about what my life is going to be like, ten years from now, God willing—not checking my phone as often as I did. To not hear or see all those people that I once followed or who once followed me. To not worry about getting into arguments with random people and having peace in my mind and my heart. To live a life without social media; that will be a life worth living for me; to keep the mystery.

I am sure by now that you thought about this, and would ask me if I ever logged back on social media? Even if it was just to snoop around? To be honest with you, I did, but to be perfectly frank with you, I regretted it instantly. Because as I said before, the addiction was waiting for me to come back. My addiction to social media will always be there waiting for me. That time I logged on to remove the rest of my old pictures, it was like jumping into an ocean with super-strong currents. It was doing it's absolute worst, trying to pull me back into the depths of its' world. As soon as I got my last pictures off, I logged off so fast and never went back.

What a nightmare! What a scary, everlasting dream. The bottom line is this; I just beg of you, the readers, not to repeat these mistakes that I had made on the devices. Do not disclose your personal lives on these platforms. Our own experiences are not for the world to know about daily. If all your social media profiles consist of pictures of rocks and flowers from all over the world; cats, and dogs, by all means, I think you will be fine. However, you would still have to be careful with how much time you spend looking at other people's profiles. That is how it sucks up your time. Keep your business to yourselves if you continue to use social media. Making yourselves very accessible on social media can cause much damage to friendships; specifically, relationships and marriages.

Keeping the mystery is what will keep life worth living. That is why when people ask questions such as, "what happens when we die?" Well, as far as the physical part, we have funerals, and then we are buried or cremated. As far as the spiritual side and the afterlife, we do not know. Even if we knew something, I believe it should be kept as a mystery. We will know eventually, right? Just understand and acknowledge that you exist on this planet. You are alive on this living rock, in a universe of magic and mystery. If we knew everything about our world, then what would be the purpose of our existence? I said this once before on social media, "*our purpose as human beings on this earth, is the greatest treasure mankind has yet to find.*" If we knew everything, that would leave no room for discovery or mystery. I believe we will always be looking for answers as to why we are here on this earth. I also think that is what makes life so fascinating to live through. I think of the mystery, the sheer magic of it all, the mystery of God, and the mystery of us human beings on this earth. But unfortunately, social media has found a way to unlock that mystery about us. Collecting our data, knowing our friendships and relationships, turning us into puppets on the strings. Transforming the world into billions of Pinocchio dolls, or should I say we have become our form of the wizard behind the curtain.

Maybe you should ask yourself, "do I believe in magic?" Even if you try to predict it, magic is unpredictable; and there is magic everywhere. The weather is magic; the rain is magic, growing trees, volcanoes, the sun, the moon, the mystery of it all is pure magic. For those of you who have children, to see them as babies, grow into a walking talking young adults. That is nothing but magic; the magic of our creator. These are the events in our lives that we cannot explain or predict, nor can we control them. Keep in mind, as I mentioned earlier, humans are guests on this earth. The earth was not made exclusively for humankind. So, there are occurrences that happen in life that are out of our league to deal with, that are unpreventable.

There will be unexpected tragedies that happen in life; that leaves us with nonexistent explanations as to why they happened. How do we handle these tragedies? We treat them how a human being could handle them. We cry it out; we talk it out, we walk it out, we hug it through, we love through others, and we cry some more. It is painfully challenging because it is so difficult to stay sane, knowing things will never be the same again. But we make it through; you will make it through. That is why it is important to always love people for who they are today. Love them for who they are today and not loving an idea of who you think they are or who they could potentially be later on in life, because you may not get a chance to see that. That is why I got the hell off of social media. Because I refused to be "liked," by random strangers, based on an idea of who I deceived people into believing I am. I would much rather be loved by the people in my actual life, for who I am today.

With all of that being said, social media is not magic. It is merely a human-made machine, a slot machine that decides who is going to be the lucky winner. There is no mystery to be kept on these platforms. The data you feed to the beast is what will have you thinking that you and your smart T.V. are in sync with each other. For example, you make a post saying, "Lion King was your favorite childhood movie." Then ten minutes later, you see the Lion King show up on one of your tv channels or an ad at least. Now is that magic? Is that a coincidence, or are social media and the internet taking your data and information, setting up the algorithms, predicting or recommending what it thinks you want to watch? I cannot tell you the number of moments I thought of a T.V. show or movie, turned on the television and saw what I was thinking about at that moment. That is not magic! The power of predictability. But who can prove that?

This is the game; this is the Matrix we are in now. If you do not seriously take a step back, open your minds, and peep the game, you just might end up addicted and controlled by these entities like I once was. Heads down, visible eyelids, hypnotized into that social media world. Unless you figure out a way to manage and maintain your usage of these things, you will end up just like me. These platforms are way too powerful, and we have way too much free will, not to be hooked, not only hooked on social media but our phones in general.

Years from now, human beings could potentially have the necks of Giraffes, bent and stretched looking down at their phones. The bottom line; the mystery of ourselves, of our lives, is for us to keep and never disclose to a virtual platform of judgment.

20 *Likes*

My Last Post (Final Thoughts)

I understand this is the world we have created for ourselves. A world of instant microwaved results of validation, comfort, worth, and being liked by random people that we will never know. You will never know half of the people who are following you on those platforms or at least stay in touch with half of them. So, why? Why hold on to the disconnect? Why hold on to something that will, yes, create some fantastic opportunities for you, but in return, will still keep you in the loop of checking your phone. Checking every five minutes, every two minutes; just to see the little "*treats*" you will get; as Jaron Lanier calls the likes and notifications; *treats*.

So many problems came from my experiences with social media. One of the issues I truly believed sparked such chaos on these platforms; is by some people who needed to be better than the next person. People had to feel more important than others. Then having celebrities and everyday people come together.

Next thing you know, people begin to compare their lives to the lives of the rich and famous, knowing there is not much comparison from a financial perspective. So, people started to pretend on social media, make everything a highlight reel, rack up on the likes, the comments, the views, and new followers.

People are so quick to post their new relationships, so excited for instant feedback and reactions. People do not even give their relationship time to marinate in life, posting a raw look at new love. To truly love someone, you must protect that love, not exploit it to the public. Social media makes people fall in love with the ideas and fantasies of who people are, and not pay attention to the real character, the real person behind those devices and platforms. One could imagine how painful a breakup could be in this world of technology and social media.

Think about it; you may take a thousand pictures with your significant other; things eventually do not work out anymore, then you break up within a year or so. You have all these posts, all these pictures of the two of you, so in love with each other. You then have to unfollow each other from your platforms. You have to remove all of those pictures, from your social media and your phone, and finally, your consciousness.

Then after that, your followers begin to realize that you have not posted a picture of your relationship in months. Now they automatically assume that you are no longer together with your partner. For women, that could bring endless amounts of messages to their profiles; a bunch of guys asking them out; now that they are single, and on the market again. Remember when there was a time if you were in a relationship, you had pictures of you and your significant other all over your room? Then if you broke up, you had to remove each photo one by one? The images are hanging on your bedroom mirror; on your door and your nightstand. Maybe that still happens in today's world. But as of now, with technology, all we do is touch these screens and hit the delete button.

What I also realized about social media is this. When you have a fall out with someone in your actual real life, for whatever reason, social media will still have you connected to that person, until either one of you decides to delete each other from those platforms. But if neither side removes each other, and you continue to see each other's posts every day. The pain, the betrayal, the mistrust will begin to grow, like cancer, which could potentially cause hate towards one another—staying connected to a disconnected real-life friendship or relationship.

There is no telling what is to come in this social media world. The type of control and power these platforms will have on these young children today, tomorrow, and the future. There was this one winter’s day; I saw two little girls, they may have been kindergartners or first graders, who were outside playing in front of their school. They were throwing little snowballs at each other. I looked at them, and I thought, "They look so happy." There they are, playing in the snow. I heard the little girl who threw the snowball at her friend, saying, "I got you! I got you!" I fear that their innocence will be robbed from them at an early age, if or when they come in contact with social media and smartphones. There was a time where kids chased each other, playing a game called "tag," whoever was "it," had to chase after someone else, tag them and say, "now you're it!" Now, we have a generation of kids who "tags" each other on their social media posts. Now the youth plays "tag" and "hashtag" with their posts. The innocent minds of the youth are being tainted with a new era of cyberbullying, hatred, negativity, suicidal tendencies, anxiety, and fear like you can never imagine.

I fear the youth will lose their individuality, their voices, their dreams, their lives, all over the world. I fear that children will just go with the flow, only agreeing with the majority of thoughts and emotions that have already been formed, and not establishing a voice and thought process of their own—looking for a way to be a superhero, by being a victim.

Is this the life that people are supposed to be living in today? Where everywhere you go, every step of the way, we are surrounded by groups of people with their heads down, deeply engaged in their phones. People being unbelievably cruel to each other via social media, at any age range. People looking for any spectacle to record, so they can post a potential viral video and see those numbers spike up their dopamine.

In this world, we are living in a world that is destined for global mental enslavement. We are enslaved by time, enslaved by our jobs, religion, money, products, enslaved by the foods we eat, politics, beauty, and now, technology and social media. I almost forgot about fear. Fear is what keeps the mental enslavement healthy, comfortable, and profitable. When African people, my ancestors, were deliberately enslaved and brought here to America. There were much business and profit in the cotton industry that was made. Profit was made on their blood, sweat, tears, and even death. I think about my ancestors, the hell they all went through, serving, and not acknowledged as human beings. Out in the plantations, picking cotton until their fingers bled, and if they did not pull enough cotton for the day, they would suffer some more—a lot more.

My ancestors have fought, died, and survived for our freedom. Unfortunately, mental enslavement has emerged through this social media world. Except for this time, it is not just African Americans who are being mentally enslaved and who are suffering. It is universal enslavement; no matter the complexion, everyone who is heavily active on these platforms are being programmed and enslaved. Absolutely everyone, the difference is you are not picking cotton; today, you are posting cotton. You may not understand me, do you? Allow me to elaborate; our data and information are the most lucrative and profitable pieces of material in the world. The information has always been the most sought-after material in the world, and we see that to this day. Our information and data will forever be profitable. Every time you post a picture, a quote, or whatever you desire, that is a piece of cotton, digital cotton that you are feeding to the machine. Sure, you will get some likes. But as long as you are on these platforms, posting that cotton, you will never be free.

What is freedom? Is it just freedom of speech? Free thinking, free-roaming of the world, free from debt, free from trouble or chaos? What is this atmosphere that we, black people, or people in general, who are feeling lockdown, are fighting and dying to achieve? I believe freedom is knowing who you are; knowing your destiny and your purposes for why God has placed you on this earth and being unapologetic about what you do with your life. Freedom is beyond the actual word; it is a privilege. Freedom is understanding that you do not need to buy something to be happy, even if you can afford it. Freedom is walking out that door every morning with your head held high, making eye contact, not just with other people, but with life all around you. The trees, the grass, the sky, the sun, everything that breathes life is freedom. Freedom is knowing that as a human, you share the world with other living beings; animals that mean us no harm. Freedom is having the option of living with or without religion. Freedom is in education. Freedom is more about a presence, a feeling, what you believe, and very little about what you buy and what you consume. But what freedom is never going to be; is you, waking up in the morning, and before you even stretch your body, turn around to kiss your significant other and say good morning, before you get up out of your bed to use the restroom, the very first thing you do is check your phones, and check your social media accounts.

That is by no way, shape, or form freedom. That is an addiction, it is mental enslavement, and quite frankly, that is insanity. But the thing is, I am not judging you, I am judging myself on this. I was addicted, I was mentally enslaved to these platforms, and quite frankly; it sailed me into a land of insanity. The only way I can ever redeem myself and make my peace with all of this is to share with you, the reader, my experience of being on social media. If I did not write this book, I would be committing a darkened sin, an act of evil by not saying a word about the possible consequences that could be waiting for you or your children; if you do not take a break at least and do some reflecting.

This world cannot go on like this; we cannot survive this way of living. Jaron Lanier said, well actually I am paraphrasing, this is not the exact quote; but Lanier mentioned, "*As long as these tech companies keep their same business models, we cannot survive if two people are trying to connect, but there is a third party behind the scenes who wish to manipulate them.*" I would like to add on to what Lanier said and say that, "we cannot be free as long as we are seeking acceptance and validation, from random strangers that we will never meet in our actual lives." If these machines were ever to stop, this world could head towards a virtual Armageddon. An Armageddon to our minds.

So, I say this to you all in these closing thoughts, I ask of you; just give it a chance. Just try to take a break. Take a break from these social media platforms. I will suggest to you the same method I used for becoming a vegan. The way I became a vegan, I stopped eating animal products one by one. But the way I started, I decided I would first stop eating animal products that were my least favorite, which was turkey. The second was pork, third being red meat, fourth being chicken, and last but not least seafood. You can apply that same method with social media. Decide which platform is your least favorite and break from that one first. Then the next month, go for the second one, then the following month, go for the third, and so on.

Now, one last time, I am not trying to tell you what to do; that is my number one rule. It is your life, your choice. What I just said was simply a suggestion, just in case you may be asking, "so, what should we do?" That is my suggestion. My overall purpose with this book is to present you with another alternative. I have stayed in touch with quite a good number of friends and family via emails or direct phone calls and text messages. I seriously doubt you would feel the need to keep in touch with hundreds, if not thousands of people's profiles daily. Missing out on someone else's life is nowhere near as disappointing than missing out on your own life and wasting time scrolling on your phone, looking at random profiles.

Now, I had to repeat myself in this book. That is because I wanted to remind you that it is still your choice. It is not for me to say to you, what is best for you. You may love social media. Social media may have changed your life. But ask yourself this question; did social media improve your life experience, or did social media give you a life? Did it give you a fake life that was better than the actual life you were living? A life filled with likes, comments, views, and followers is not a life worth remembering. It may be a life worth living to very few, but it rarely will be a life to remember. What will you remember if you feed more of your memories and knowledge to the machines that other people have designed for business, instead of feeding the machines that God has already designed within you; your brain and your heart? A mind that will help you reminisce a life that was worth living, and a heart that will cherish the people in your life, that you love the most—the life and times to remember.

When I think about it, I do not recall having that many dreams while I was on social media, and when I say dreams, I mean the dreams we have while we sleep. I do not recall having many of those dreams. Probably because I never slept much, I was so preoccupied scrolling up and down my phones at the wee hours of the night. Building up all of that anxiety and not even understanding why I was waking up every morning depressed, feeling isolated, alone, and anxious.

The numbers made me numb to reality. The number of friends I had on FB, but not all were real friends. The number of followers who I did not follow back. Keeping the number of my followers higher than the number of people I followed, just to look as if I was of importance. I was giving my soul away for numbers that meant absolutely nothing—putting my personal business out there for the public to judge and deliver their two cents. I was not winning; I was losing. I was losing my mind, my common sense, my integrity, and possibly lost the love of my life. I lost much more than I gained from social media. I pulled the handle on the slot machine, and I simply just did not hit the jackpot.

So, the way I feel about social media is this; I am not entirely against social media; I am against the system that is designed for it. I am not saying, not even thinking, that if you continue to use social media, that you are a fool. That is not the impression I want this book to display. Yes, I know social media can offer some real-life opportunities. Some people have found their true love through social media; that was their jackpot. But like the slot machine, people take their winnings and go right back and play with the money they just won, then lose all of their winnings and then some. Then afterward, they are completely empty on the inside.

So, when people who then post pictures of their relationship with their true love, then get random strangers involved in their personal life; that is how they begin to lose the spark, the magic, and mystery that their relationship once had when they first found each other, which could then taint their relationship and break them apart.

Social media from afar looks beautiful, but the deeper and deeper you get into it, the more dangerous it becomes; and you feel the pull. It is like the ocean; from the beach, the sea looks so beautiful. But when you start to go into the ocean waters, that ocean current pulls you in, takes you into the deep, and then you are in danger. All I would genuinely say to you is simply be careful; be mindful of what you post, know your following as best as you can.

I did not write this book in an attempt to be famous. I do not need to be a celebrity. I just want to celebrate life the way we were designed to celebrate it; with love, creativity, appreciation to God our creator, to be grateful for whatever time we have on this earth and having beautiful memories to store more in our minds and hearts, than in our electronic devices and social media.

Some of you may be thinking, "who is Jordan Wells?" I will simply answer that by saying, "Jordan Wells is me! I am Jordan Wells." I do not define myself with many words because I am a man of very few words. I do not define my life, my achievements, or myself by words or numbers. I define myself by my actions. By my characteristic traits. For the people who I have interacted with, befriended in life. I am sure many of them would say I am quiet. But they will remember the way I treated them. They will remember me through my actions and not through words.

There is only one number that I will always look forward to in this life. Every time it gets higher, and that number is my age. The one thing about getting older, the number of our age, it will never decline. We cannot get any younger in this life. We may have mastered looking more youthful, but truth be told, our age never lies. The number of our age will continue to go up, never down. That is probably the only number that rises; that I am forever grateful for achieving.

I honestly believe that there is a beautiful life to be lived without social media. I am living proof of that, along with many others who probably never opened an account. But for me to be on those platforms for all those years, addicted, and then to delete them all. That was a miracle for me. I had my years of social media, and I do not need or want anymore. As an actor, I am aware that it is part of some celebrities' contracts, to have a social media presence, and to be marketable. Well, I am just going to have to be one of those actors, who pursues his "social media-free" acting career, without compromise. Because as long as I live, I will never log back on to social media.

Again, I refuse to blame personally, CEO Mark Zuckerberg, and his co-founders. I do not blame Jack Dorsey and his partners. I do not point the finger at Kevin Systrom, Mike Krieger, Evan Spiegel, or Steve Chen and his team. I blame none of them for my addiction to social media; I blame no one. I did not know the power that these platforms potentially could and did have over me. But you live, and you learn in this game of life. Also, I am not crying victim here; I started using these devices as a young teenager, who did not know any better. What is coincidental about social media is that most of the founders of these tech empires, started these companies while they were teenagers. Perhaps they were young and naïve to what impact it could have, along with the dangers of it too.

I do not know what you, the reader, will think about all of this. Maybe some of you will relate to me, and others will not understand. Perhaps some do not believe social media causes people to become addicted. Perhaps it does not affect some people in that way, or it just does not affect you. I only hope that you at least open your mind and think. Think before you post, think before you like, and think before you watch. I hope that if or when you feel that you cannot get off of these platforms, or if you find yourself addicted, that you catch it and quit it. To the young ones, one last thing; you do not need social media to succeed in this world. Do you know what you absolutely, truly need to succeed in this world? An education; period!

I am sure that whoever reads this book will have their reviews and opinions on it. People will have their take. You will have your agreements and disagreements, your likes and dislikes. By all means, pick it apart, dissect it, find discoveries about yourself within it. I am sure you may discover and envision things that I myself did not see. Your constructive criticism and your opinions are welcomed. I, for one, will not be able to see those reviews or see what people will have to say about this book. Because I, fortunately, am not on social media anymore. I logged off, never to return. Will you?

Conclusion

Let Me Tell You

Tupac Amaru Shakur. I am sure whoever reads this knows who I am talking about by now. For those who do not, I will just say to you, Tupac was way ahead of his time; in a short period of time. He breathed life on this earth for only twenty-five years. There was magic with this brother. He took words and created these stories; that was pure, cruel, raw, and mysterious. His work made me think. It made me acknowledge what it means to be a black African man in America. A very misunderstood man he was. Tupac was taken from the world twenty-three years ago. Yet, his voice remains powerful, alive if you will, in today's society. To this day, I still see many people walking around wearing a Tupac shirt. He said in an interview once, "*I am not saying I am going to change the world, but I guarantee that I will spark the brain that will change the world.*" I always asked myself when I was younger if I would be the chosen one. I do not know. Perhaps I will find out someday. I wonder what a man like Tupac Shakur would do or say, had he been alive today and on social media? How would Jim Morrison use social media if he was around?

I would not know really. I would find that to be very interesting to see both of these men, two of my favorite poets, on these platforms. However, I believe they would have done the same thing I did; they would have escaped it. They would have been wise enough to know what dangers come with it, especially being a rebel, like those two men were. They both would probably share some of their thoughts, their poetry, and then after a while, just disappear from it. As I mentioned; Tupac was twenty-five when he was assassinated in Las Vegas in the year 1996; and Jim died in Paris, France, in the year 1971; at the age of twenty-seven. Two very young ages, two young men who had a lot more to offer to the world. So much more potential to capture a much more significant mark on this earth. But something interesting about the two. Jim died on July 3rd, 1971. Tupac was born on June 16th, 1971, just three weeks before Jim's death. As one genius is born, the other exits; in the same year, three weeks apart.

I talk about these two men, not out of worshipping them, but with much admiration. I have learned a lot from both of these young men. As musicians, as poets, as iconic figures that I believe will be around for a very long time. Some of my favorite lines Jim wrote in his song "*Riders on The Storm*," "*Into this house we're born, into this world we're thrown. Like a dog without a bone, an actor out on loan, riders on the storm.*" Those lines, those lyrics, they just pull me in, along with so many others from The Doors. My favorite Tupac song is "*Hail Mary*," that I talked about before. This song is from his first posthumous album that was released, "*Makaveli Tha Don: Killuminati: The 7 Day*

Theory." It was almost like he was preparing himself for what was to come. That is what I learned about being prepared, with anything in life. To be prepared is to be an individual. To go your way in life is the ultimate key. These two men went their way; they made their way in this world, and in return, they will always live on through their legacy. They will never be forgotten. Tupac and Jim have helped me; they inspired me to think, and to go my own way. Escaping the social media world; was me breaking on through to the other side, which is another song by The Doors.

I have prepared myself to go my own way; I have also prepared myself with being misunderstood. As an individual, I have been misunderstood my whole life. Some people may not understand how an African American, like myself, survived and made it out. I made it out of my environment without the temptations of drinking, smoking, drugs, criminal records, becoming a vegan, and deleting all of my social media accounts. You may think I am a monk by now, right? Well, my motto about this life; is we must live it until the very end, and "if you want to be a better person, then just be a better person." Take the necessary steps that are needed to improve your life, to see different results. I understand addictions are brutal. But your will, plus God's will, is mightier than any addiction can handle. You must first realize you have a problem, acknowledge that it is a problem, then practice a solution to heal your problem. You have weight problems; practice not eating those foods that are putting a lot of weight on you. Whatever your problems may be, practice some solutions. You will see much needed, motivational results.

I remember when I was around seventeen years old, I went to a presentation of this phone company. One of the CEO's of the company was talking, and he said, "*If you do what everyone else does, you are going to get what everyone else gets*." That changed my life from that point on. I always kept that in mind. I did not even hear anything else that was said that night; I listened to what I needed to hear. That made sense to me. But I was disappointed in myself for letting twelve years go by, using those social media apps like everyone else. I did not apply that message that was given to me that night at the presentation. Not saying that message was meant explicitly for getting off of social media, but the message was clear; do not be a follower, lead yourself, and be an individual.

I hope I did not confuse you, the reader of this book, or to spoil the fun you do have with social media. I understand; when you achieve something great, it feels so great to post and share it with others. I know that social media has become this pictorial calendar of birthdays, holidays, and events that keeps us feeling alive and up to date. I get it, I have been there. But my only issue with it all is how you will continuously be trying to figure out what is next. "What will be the next thing I need to post, what is the next thing I have to achieve?" To get that rush of dopamine; over and over and over again.

All of this for the approval and validation of strangers? You do not need it. Just because there are billions of people in the world, it does not mean you are obligated to befriend as many people as you can. Not all of us will get along; not all of us will be kind to one another even though we should be kind to one another. But actually, you must protect yourself from other people. Because let me tell you; social media has done its' damage to the world but be no mistake, social media is not the innovator. It is not the pioneer of chaos, racism, greed, sexism, addiction, or any other issues that make our world dark and corrupted. Social media is just a baby compared to the other toxins and distractions that flows through the veins of our society.

One of those toxins I am referring to is guns. Guns were here way before social media. When I think about guns and the violence they continue to cause in America, I ask myself, why? Why are guns such a necessity in this country? Why does America love guns so much? That is when it hit me. Guns, to this day, are still the quickest way to death. Guns are not cancer; they are not HIV or AIDS, nor are they drugs you can overdose from, and die. All it takes is one bullet, and it is all over. Plus, guns are what helped build America.

I would say that guns were too powerful, too quick for Native Americans to go to war with the Europeans, and to win. Too powerful for African people who were enslaved. Without guns, there would be no United States of America today, as we know it. No guns, no America. Guns are America's true religion. As long as there is the United States of America, guns will never cease to exist. Guns are the roots that helped America grow. It is what gave America life, and just like life, it will find a way to spread and grow. Mass and school shootings are just more ways for guns to breathe more life. It is just an ironic tragedy that for guns to live, we must die. Seeing mass shootings being filmed live on FB, post going up about school shootings, terrifying the parents and students of America. I believe that violence is deliberately exploited in America. Just to keep inspiring the criminally insane to produce more violent crimes, which then eventually produces more books, movies, and documentaries of the criminally insane. To create the potential of inspiring people into a world of criminalization, and that is now out of control. But that is for another book too.

One last thing I want to say, and then I will conclude this journey that I guided you through. If you decide to take a little break from your accounts, let me just tell you; you are a hero. You are a hero because you have reduced your chances of feeding the machine. It has no real ways of loving you by giving you the little digital favors every time you post something. You give your mind a chance to recover and not have it programmed. By not scrolling up and down news feeds, seeing a whole bunch of skullduggeries of posts, that would turn your mind into an apocalypse. You are a hero because you care about yourself. You care about your mental health, your precious time, and the fact that you are willing to give up these platforms, where random followers are judging you.

Do me a favor when you take that break. Find a beautiful park, or lake, or somewhere by the water. I will even settle for a swimming pool, just somewhere outdoors, where you can look up at the sky. There is a song by one of the greats; the Late great Miles Davis. Miles has a song called "*Mr. Pastorious*," from his second to last album, "*Amandla*." There are no lyrics, of course, just the genius of his playing on the trumpet, with Marcus Miller on the bass. When you are outside, wherever you are, have a seat somewhere; play this song with your headphones on and just listen to it. It will clear your mind and your consciousness and just put you in a peaceful state of being. Do not think of anything else; just hear Miles. Do not think about your past, your breakups, no likes, no comments, no views or subscribers, no friend requests, and no followers. I promise you will not regret it.

Now, if it is the nighttime, there is another song I would like you to listen to as well. There is another song, by my favorite film composer, Thomas Newman. Newman composed films such as "*The Shawshank Redemption*," "*The Green Mile*," "*American Beauty*," "*Cinderella Man*," and my favorite, "*Pay It Forward*." There is a song Newman made on the soundtrack of the film "*Pay It Forward*" called "*I forgive you*." There is something about this song that puts me into this mysterious dream world. A dream world where I feel like I am in the cold night desert, with the moon shining bright, and the song just echoes throughout the desert. If you can, listen to those two songs when you are on your own time, outside, or wherever you are. Listen to Miles Davis, listen to Thomas Newman, and listen to that inner voice in you that is saying, "Bravo!" "Bravo!"

You may not get it or understand at first. But one day I am sure you will. One day I am sure you will remember what I say in this book. Just know that it is up to you. It is always up to you. To have a life with privacy, without the pressure of sharing your business, your happiness, love, goals, and dreams. If you want to share anything with this world, take that beautiful smile that God has blessed you with and share it with others.

THANK-YOUS

If you have come this far in the book, let me start by saying thank you. Thank you for taking some of your precious time away from your phone and social media and used your valuable time to read my book. I just really had something to say, something that I feel is important to share with the world, especially the youth and the next generation of children to come. The children who will be born deep into this social media world. A world of smartphones, tablets, videos, posts, and numbers. I have faith that this will reach people from all over the world, who will take a moment to realize what is going on with themselves.

To give thanks to some people, I would like to thank Mrs. Walkins, who has been like a second mother to me. I want to thank Marion Bell III, Lawrence Woods, Coach Will, Coach Watkins, Coach Bo, Coach Saint, David Malyszko, and Shea Richardson. I want to thank once again, my college English professor, who I took several courses with, professor Henry "Hank" Stewart. For educating me on the craft of writing, how to be expressive in my book, and fearlessly poetic. I want to thank some other professors that I had the pleasure to work with, who helped me open up more and expressed myself artistically. Those people are Stephen Davis, who I still stay in contact with and maintain a good relationship with to this day. I want to thank Devon Vialva, Lea Antolini-Lid, Carl Wallnau, Tiffany Kushner, Kisty Dixon, Norman Cetuk, Dr. Ken Autore, Kathleen Naasz, Dr. McHugh, Professor Bachstein, Neil

Andrito, and the list can go on and on. I want to thank everyone who I had the pleasure to work with at the Shakespeare Theatre of New Jersey and Jagger; you all know who you are. I have to thank two writers/directors; Leslye Headland and Tracy Oliver, who I had the pleasure of working with on the set of the T.V. shows "Russian Doll" and "First Wives Club." It was their brilliant writing, that was the spark of inspiration, for me to write one day. I did not know I would be writing a book, so I thank them. There are two others who I want to thank for changing my perception of life and how I will be living it from now on. Two men by the name of Joshua Fields Millburn and Ryan Nicodemus, who are self-proclaimed "Minimalists." I see myself living such a lifestyle, a life where I only surround myself with people and things that gives real meaning and value to me. They are on to something; as I go my own way in life, I will use the philosophy that Millburn mentioned, "love people and like things." I want to also give thanks to Damon "Dame" Dash for sparking the fire in me to be self-sufficient.

I would also like to thank God, the creator, my family, my mother, and my father for bringing me into this world. I want to thank my real friends; you know who you are. Thank you all for the love and support since the very beginning. I want to leave you with something special. I have for you fifteen poems; some I wrote over nine years ago; when I was receiving acting training at the Shakespeare Theatre of New Jersey. These poems will be a spark to my poetry book; that I will publish sometime in the following year. Thanks to you all for your time. Hopefully this book has made a difference in your life, as well as others. Take great care, and God bless!

The Lost Daughter (1/31/11)

She wakes up;
As she walks out to her balcony,
To bear witness of this beautiful morning.
She feels reborn,
She feels miraculously safe.
She lives one day at a time
From an unbearable tragic life.
A life no human being should have ever lived,
Not even an animal.
Once upon her time;
She had a mother, a father.
They loved her more than
Anyone could ever be loved.
They loved her excessively.
One late night;
Her mother and father argued.
Her at eight years old,
Hears her mother scream "Divorce,"
A word she does not understand.
Not much later; Big bang!
A Bang that changes her universe,
Her life, forever.
The daughter hears hysterical screams,
She runs to her two parents,
To find only one still breathing.
The daughter sees "suicide,"
Another word that this 8-year-old does not understand.
Her mother takes her out of the
Disturbing sight,
She calls for her father to wake up;
Wake up from his 357. Magnum coma,
But he is gone.
The daughter cries tears of confusion as
Her mother cries tears of sudden guilt.

Time goes by; 3 years.
Mother weds again.
Through the mother's eyes;
A husband, a lover.
Through daughter's eyes;
A monster with an evil mission.
One night her mother is not home.
The daughter on the couch,
Sitting beside her, her nightmare.
Out of nowhere, he begins to say things to her.
Things that an 11-year-old should never hear,
Things he would only say to her mother.
His words transformed into touches,
Sick, perverted touches.
At her innocent young age;
She does not get an epiphany of
What is going on, but she's not comfortable.
As she tries to leave,
His touches transformed into grabs,
She screams and screams,
Yet no one hears her,
As if she is a ghost.
He drags her into her room,
Slams and locks the door,
With him inside there with her.
No words ever created,
Can explain what evil went on in that room,
Or what he did to her.
Morning comes, she sees her mother.
The daughter does not mention a word,
Not even a letter of what happened to her.
More time goes by:
Her mother begins to wonder
Why her daughter retires for the night
On the couch rather than her bed.
So many tears were cried,
So many frightening nightmares,

So many more of his demonic caresses,
His derange ambition for rape.
She cannot take it anymore.
She cannot stay in her room,
She cannot tell her mother,
She cannot tell anyone; she is lost.
Another late night;
She hears her mother arguing
With her devilish husband,
A Deja vu of the night four years ago.
Her mother screams "divorce" again,
A word the daughter still does not understand,
But is expecting to hear the big bang.
She hears the big bang,
She hears it 4 times.
The daughter is shocked at first.
But she is relieved, thinking her nightmare is gone.
She begins to realize that this night
is different from the other.
She does not hear her mother scream,
Yet she hears laughter.
She runs to the room,
Expecting to see her mother standing tall,
Her mother is lying dead
With the four big bangs pierced in her body.
She sees "murder," another word she does not understand.
Her nightmare stands there
With his drunken voice, saying humorously;
"Four wasted years equals four bullets."
She thought her nightmare was over,
He just got stronger.
She sees her mother being thrown
Away as if she is garbage.
He takes her away,
She begins a devastating journey into
A very hell bound, dark world.
God help her, please help her.

She lived with her nightmare for
Many more unimaginable years.
He turned her into a sex slave,
Into a drug-addicted prostitute,
Locked up in his basement prison,
Those abusive nights and horrific years.
Yet from all those years,
She gained some knowledge.
She now understands the meaning of "divorce,"
The definition of suicide,
The definition of murder.
She had to escape her nightmare,
This lost daughter had to find her way out.
She had to make a decision,
She had a question like Hamlet.
Either she lives by committing murder,
Killing her nightmare of a stepfather.
Or she dies by committing suicide.
She made her decision.
He comes to her for his
Night of pleasure, with a pair of scissors,
With a vision of her with shorter hair.
She sees the scissors; she sees her moment.
She sees her chance to escape her nightmare.
As he goes to chip away at her hair,
She uses the knowledge she gained as
A sex slave, seducing-him, making him
Feel more comfortable.
Her plot worked beautifully.
She grabbed the scissors,
And with all her might,
Plus, the strength of God,
She stabbed away.
Now she is standing tall.
All she had to say to him
During the last beats of his
Satanic black heart was;

"Seven years of horrific torture,
Seven years of this horrible nightmare,
Equals seven stabs, plus the power of Karma."
No one could probably imagine
How this young girl survived.
Living through seven years of molestation,
Seven years of abuse; of rape.
Suffering the instant loss of her
Father, of her mother,
Being kidnapped, being lost.
Her troubled time is past her now.
Now at her adult age;
She is healing, slowly but surely.
She is filtering all the poisons from her body.
Yet she still feels somewhat lost.
She lost the love she once had from her parents.
People would wonder what will happen to this girl.
Is she going to be alright,
Will she live on and be happy?
What is next for this lost daughter?
Tomorrow, I guess.

"I would like to dedicate this poem to all of the women, the young girls, all of the lost daughters around the world. The women who have endured such heinous, traumatic, and unforgettable pain; of verbal, physical, and sexual abuse. There are much better days waiting for you." -Jordan Wells

Imagine (Dedicated to John Lennon) (11/7/10)

Imagine there's no music.

No life-changing lyrics,

No hypnotizing harmonies for the lives of billions.

Imagine no oceans for the world,

No surfers, no water polo, no slave ships; no Titanic.

No hurricanes formed for destruction.

Imagine there's no money,

No need for investments,

No need for banks,

No inflation or recession.

Just imagine no planes;

Ritchie Valens could still be saying "La Bamba,"

Rocky Marciano could still be fighting,

In the 87th round of his life, still undefeated.

Imagine no horror,

No classics from Bram Stoker or Mary Shelley.

Imagine there are no books,

The forest of trees would survive, yes,

But the forest of knowledge would burn to ashes.

Imagine there's no paint or brushes,

No Mona Lisa, no presidential portraits,

No love for the world of art.
Imagine there's no acting,
As if there were no Oscars,
No Tony awards to win.
The work of William Shakespeare would be lost.
Imagine there are no stars,
The face of space being cleared
Of that shinning acne.
Imagine there's no racism.
I'm trying to imagine that,
But it is hard to do.
Living in a world where we are not
Known as black, white, yellow,
Red, or orange; you are known
And loved as human beings
Imagine; John Lennon still breathing.
Never mind the Beatles,
Never mind the interviews,
Never mind the cameras and autographs.
Imagine John walking with his beloved
Yoko in Central Park, on a 2010 day.
Imagine John seeing his
Beautiful, beautiful, beautiful, beautiful boys
Grow up to be men.

Imagine the world giving peace a chance.

This divine man once said

"All you need is love."

The truth is, all we needed was John Lennon.

I Am Gun

I am the quickest killer ever known to man,

I can kill anyone or anything, give me your hand.

My bullet soldiers are what I use,

I can order them in any direction, but you must choose.

I was born and made in China; in case you didn't know,

Now I'm everywhere, like water, I flow.

Don't know my exact date of birth, know I'll never die,

Killed millions since day one; no remorse, I don't cry.

I am a Hollywood mogul, an idol to the music of rap,

I don't know why I'm so unique; I'm giving the living a dirt nap.

If only you can see peoples' faces once I show them mine,

It's like they can't move, can't talk, frozen in a non-Disney time.

I am a way of life, or should I say death,

I observed so many lives taking their last breath.

I am the master instrument of instant incidents,

Mass and school shootings, innocent bodies, bloody craters and dents.

Some call me protection, keeping me in their nightstands;

Others call me a weapon if I fall into the wrong hands.

Ban me, have me deported; I'll leave and never come back;

Been through too many wars, genocide, suicides, deadly attacks.

I've seen it all, till this day I can't believe this life is real;

I don't understand why people use me to kill.

America, oh America; why do you love me so much?

Is it the sounds, the smell, the taste, the grip, or the touch?

Shootings every single day; some survive, some win;

I always wondered why my trigger is shaped like the Amazon grin.

To the good, I am bad, to the bad I am good

With my double-barrel shotgun eyes, I clearly can see we're all misunderstood.

(2/13/14; edited on 12/23/19)

Late for School

Break of dawn, the birds are singing,

Alexa, Alexa, stop that ringing.

Showered, clothes, keys, out the door

No time to make breakfast, running to the nearest store.

Grabbed a bagel, enlarged with cream cheese

"Hold it! You're a dollar short;" "I'll pay you back, oh please, oh please!"

Already took a bite; "okay, okay,"

A handful of napkins, out the door, on his way.

Rubs on his pocket, there is no phone

Ouch with a curse word, like E.T, he goes home.

Running and running, school started, he's an hour late

Tardiness equals detention; that's great! That's great!

Unlocks the door, up the stairs, his phone is on the bed

Saw a post on social media, school shooting, at least eight are dead.

Knees buckled; eyes rolled to the back of his head

His best friend in the entire world; my God, he is dead.

A tear diving off the cliff of his cheekbone

To think his life was spared because of the absence of a cell phone.

Mother called in panic; he's safe, she's glad

But that best friend I told you about; was his teacher, his dad.

"This is in no way, trying to make light of the mass and school shooting epidemics that are taking place not just in America, but all over the world. I am simply addressing these traumatic times that we are now living in so that they are not forgotten, and hopefully not repeated in the future."

-Jordan Wells

Little Boy in the Winter Woods

A young child,
Lost in a land of snowy trees.
As he walks, he counts the trees, beyond his ten little touches,
The boy grows worried at the count of the 100th tree.
He begins to run,
Screaming and crying out his favorite word, "mommy!"
The Sun begins to slow motion down
The stairs of the horizon as the moon nights it up.
The boy lies down on the ground
That's covered with imposter sugar.
The coldness turns his tears
To frost on his face,
His calls for mommy begin to shorten,
As wells as his breath.
He begins to sing a song
That his mother sings to him,
A song called wishful stars.
As he sings, he looks up at the sky,
Searching for a wishful star.
A star is what he quickly finds,

Makes a wish to be back with his warm, tender loving mommy.

His body defeats insomnia and begins to sleep.

Time goes by; he opens his eyes.

He sees the Sun,

He sees his window,

He sees his pillow, his blanket,

His bed, his toys, his night light.

The boy no longer calls for his mommy,

She comes in with morning hugs and kisses.

The boy then realizes he was

Not in a land of frozen trees and sparkly cream.

He was in the land of an unsolicited dream.

(12/9/10)

A Present Night Tale

Feeling depress with nothing
To feel depressed about right now.
Feeling as blue as the sky,
The sky that I'm looking at now.
I look continuously, and I see a star,
The only star in this night sky.
Maybe this star is looking right back at me,
Feeling the same way as I,
With no other star to talk to in the universe.
I talked to this star, discoursed a conversation with my eyes,
Consistent looking while the star lingers in
The clear night sky, like a tattoo on a transparent body.
I ask for the star's name,
"Pick a name," is what my eyes read.
I paused in my brain for a moment,
As the electronic birds fly across the clear sky;
"Night tale" is what I call my friend.
For this night be a tale
That is beyond unforgettable.
I may never see my friend;
Ever again, a pity feeling.

Yet I have the words of memories,

Written down for safekeeping.

An impossible journey to touch her, embrace her.

A bridge of billions of miles that can't be used,

Oh, how I would give anything to hold my friend at this very moment.

The best that can be hoped for,

The soul of my friend shooting down

Into that special one, who's eyes twinkle

As much as she's twinkling now.

May then the miles swoop down to inches,

May I then be able to touch her, hug her, and love her more.

But until that time, I take my unfortunate leave

Of my beloved night tale.

(8/8/10)

Makaveli (Dedicated to Tupac Amaru Shakur)

Look into his eyes.

The same eyes that read hundreds of books,

Thousands of words.

He drowned his sponged brain

In an ocean of literature and knowledge.

Born LPC, look it up, like a prayer.

We see a man whose perceived struggle,

That felt concrete pain,

And lived and lingered in years of poverty.

We see a legend that was tragically misunderstood.

An African American prophet,

A shinning serpent with a voice of masculine eloquence.

We see his body become a tattoo museum,

We see his body become a target.

Five close ones, plus a case, equals his suicidal thoughts.

Time goes by; he sells millions to millions of inquiring minds.

He seeks ambition and revenge,

He engraves more ink on his flesh.

Listen as you hear this Black Panther

Growling lyrics for a revolution.

As you read across his belly,

America's society will see that

The **H**ate **U** **G**ive

Little **I**nfants **F**25ks **E**veryone.

A definition of his diagnosis.

A virologist artist looking to cure

The demonic diseases of

A very ill America,

An imperfect world.

A past he cannot escape,

A death he faced, too young.

Imagine if his heart

Was still pumping today.

Perhaps he would have met his unborn child,

Maybe he would have won an Oscar,

Perhaps he would have become the President,

I think he would have changed the world.

Tupac!... Tupac!... Tuuupaaaaccccc!!!

(12/7/10)

A Lover's Ghost

I'm not here anymore.
Just once I want to touch you,
Hold you tighter than any anaconda ever could.
Since I was dismissed from you,
I've been up there crying hurricanes
While you're down here crying oceans.
I wish that God could let me kiss you again,
Make love to you just one last time.
One marital year with you was a light-year far from enough.
I see you, but you can't see me;
Like a vampire's reflection in a mirror.
I hear you, but you can't listen to me,
A death so sudden, it was like a blink of an eye.
The death of my body happened,
Yet my never-ending love for you is immortal.
Please evaporate the tears from your eyes.
When I see you feeling pain,
I'm feeling torture like never before.
Please don't carry hate in your body because of my early demise.
God called for potential angels;

I couldn't decline the offer.
I guess it was a "once in a lifetime" opportunity.
Don't be angry with me.
Dismiss the tears from your face,
Close your innocent eyes and listen
As I channel into your brain,
We shall rendezvous in your dreams.
Now you can see me;
Now you can hear me clearly.
I miss you baby,
God heavenly kidnapped me,
Didn't become a hostage but became an angel.
No ransom in the world could bring me back.
My flesh, my blood, my body was exiled from your life.
But my soul is in sacred storage,
Our good times, best times are memories;
Tattooed on our minds.
I think about our child that we will never have,
I think about our anniversaries that we will never have.
I think about your day of judgment;
The day when you close your eyes for good
And the doors of your body open for your soul to exit.
Before you wake from your dream,
Know that I will be waiting for you at that light,

Were we shall assemble at the golden gates.

You deserve to live and linger in years of happiness,

But that day will reach you.

When that day comes, then will our kisses,

Our embraces, and our best times will be for all eternity.

I love you baby! Wake up.

Come Together

Let's save the human race once and for all;

The babies, the children; never too late to shine.

Los árboles de todo el mundo

Afeitado de la faz de la tierra.

Οι ωκεανοί, το υγρό περιβάλλον της ζωής,

Δίχτυα και γάντζους. Φιλέτα mignon και υδράργυρος στις φλέβες σας.

Tiere sind dem Menschen versklavt;

Tauschen Sie Ihre Teller aus, bevor es zu spät ist.

Ils crient à l'aide; on crie pour le goût,

Si formidable pour nos langues; si horrible pour notre anatomie.

私たちの脳はそんなに嫌いです、どこで考えていますか？

良い行動は私たちの社会には存在しません。

お互いが前払いするのを助けてください。

우리는이 집에 손님입니다

최악의 기물 파손, 지구가이 보편적 인 무덤에서 돌고있다

، أنظر إلى الشمس مرة أخرى ؛ إنها تفتقد وجهك

.تشعر بالغيرة من الهواتف التي تحل محلها

Materiaal vir almal; koop dit alles;

Vakansies het 'n prostitusie-ring geword.

ნუ დაკარგავთ მთელ თქვენს ფულს; ცდილობს შეიძინოს ყველას ხედვა,

ნუ დაკარგავთ თქვენს დროს; მოციმციმე სათვალეები ამ მბზინავი სათვალეებით.

改变主意改变世界；

我们可以做到这一点； 一次只有一个主意。

Imagjinoni të mos keni më dete të zi, asnjë qiell të ndotur;

Asnjë mish i kafshëve nuk u riemërua qentë e nxehtë dhe hamburgerët.

Niente pistole, o mio Dio, quello sarebbe il giorno;

Nessun proiettile che atterra attraverso i corpi dell'umanità.

If you have made it this far; that means you care;

But do not ignore this warning; don't you dare.

23 1 11 15   21 16!

Momma Gave Him Life; The Judge Gave Him Life

Momma gave him life; in her arms as he was a baby,

The judge gave him life; God no; his wife just had a baby.

Momma gave him life; crying late night tears in his crib,

The judge gave him life; crying late night tears in a cage, looks like terminator's ribs.

Momma gave him life; his first steps as he drools and grins,

The judge gave him life, his first steps walking in the pen for his sins.

Momma gave him life; says she'll be right back,

The judge gave him life, slash on his face, late-night attack.

Momma gave him life; momma's not here,

The judge gave him life, one eye open, so he's not blinded by fear.

Momma gave him life; momma was killed,

The judge gave him life; his mission must be fulfilled.

Momma gave him life; he has to find the killer,

The judge gave him life; he's now the accused killer.

Momma gave him life; he had a 45 and shovel; pop, pop, pop, POP!

The judge gave him life; I got your 45; ORDER! ORDER! STOP!

Momma gave him life; he misses her so much,

The judge gave him life; he's numb to the world, completely out of touch.

Momma gave him life; she rendezvouses to his dreams saying, "I miss you,"

The judge gave him life; CO says someone wants to see you.

Momma gave him life; momma said in a dream; “it'll all be over son.”

The judge gave him life; the lawyer told him his time here is done.

Momma gave him life; the killer was his dad

The judge gave him life, dear God; this is disturbingly bad.

Momma gave in life; dad touched the 45 before son did

The judge gave him life; your dad's prints were all over the gun; his gun, his bid.

Momma gave him life; “you will be freed my son, no more prison, no more hurt.”

The judge gave him life; he said, "I'll be home soon, as long as I don't mention I already buried the bastard; piece by piece in the dirt."

What's A Kanye? (05/08/2018)

What's a Kayne without a voice,
Telling the world slavery was just a choice.
A genius mind talking hoodwinked reckless,
Brother forgot our people were in shackles, not a diamond neckless.
What's a Kayne without the eyes,
Free thinking delivers nothing but pricey lies.
Ye screaming "Make America Great Again,"
While fans are praying for him to make a registration late again.
What's a Kanye without a brain,
Calling our brother insane,
When he's lost in the wilderness of fortune and fame.
It can happen to anyone,
No telling what you'd do, walking in the Yezzys of a motherless son.
What's a Kanye without the ears,
Hearing the teacup, seeing the tears.
What's a Kanye without a heart,
A mother and son forever separated, miles apart.
People calling him crazy, bipolar; the ultimate coon,
But how would you feel; waking in the coldest winter night,

Thinking of his best friend, who was gone too soon.
What's a Kanye without a story,
Fighting for his soul and repentance, God be the glory.
What's a Kanye without Roc-a-fella,
Friendships founder; weak propella.
Oops! I said propella; I meant propeller,
You didn't see that, Helen Keller.
What's a Kanye without tomorrow;
A legend, an icon, millions coming together in sorrow.
What is a Kanye without,
Never mind, like Kurt.

ACIREMA (Ak-her-Rheem-ma) (08/3/18)

A wealthy father, Dr. Slavery,

A mother with the looks, Ms. Racism.

A match made in Hell,

In the bed, they go.

Conceived a newborn, what is her name?

Acirema! Put a mirror to her and say her name.

Born with mental issues,

Her parents taught: her parents poisoned.

Red blood in her veins,

White skin blankets her flesh,

Blue eyes, oh she cries for help.

Still young, slowly evolving, abnormal progression.

Faces, faces, of all human races,

misplacements of lost tribes; goodness gracious.

She's rich, she's armed, and she's pregnant with a belly of economics;

But who is the father?

Incest relationship with her dad,

Dr. Slavery has gone mad.

Baby is born; what is her name?

"Mentalia Enslavement" is what they named her,

Three hundred million babysitters,

Silence! Don't wake her, she's sleeping,

Or are we the ones who are sleep?

GOD & SATAN (1/17/14)

God: The time has come for us to talk; Jesus is coming forward to once again make his mark,

Satan: You disease us with Jesus, your time is too late, the earth will flood with eternal dark.

God: Your plan will fail, putting an end to your wicked spell;

Satan: My plans are in order, can't you tell, welcome to my kingdom of pure hell.

God: Those souls are mines to keep, not yours;

Satan: Then, why such curiosity of me? Always knocking on my doors.

God: You feed them poison, so swiftly to tell a lie;

Satan: They sell me their souls, so promptly, I shall buy.

God: I will end your demonic contracts, stop your evil deals

Satan: Stop me if you dare, if you will; the news is on, I see more kills.

God: You think you have control because you influenced to make a gun?

Satan: I know I have control because my way is so much fun.

God: This universe I will heal; this world I will fix,

Satan: My worshipping patients will only come to their Dr. Six, Six, Six.

God: You think you're so unique, so divine, so funny.

Satan: I think I have more believers than you, by the love and power of money.

God: You're responsible for wars, drugs, AIDS; what's next?

Satan: Hmmm. World War 3, legalize coke and weed, metastasize unprotected sex.

God: You were an angel, why did you choose to fall?

Satan: You knew I was too greedy; it was a must that I have it all.

God: Look at what you did; yet there's more evil you want to achieve?

Satan: No, I made an offer they couldn't refuse; they ask, they shall receive.

God: What will you do? What other sadistic plans are you going to sell?

Satan: Sorry, confidential plans; my leaders under oath will soon show, never tell.

God: Just like the plan of those hijacked planes?

Satan: Yes! Oh, how I pleasure evil thoughts dancing in their brains.

God: You dare show your flaming face in the towers on that September 11th day?

Satan: I was happy as HELL; I wanted to come out and play.

God: You may be strong; but I am much mightier, much stronger;

Satan: You may be loved, but fear is what lasts longer.

God: You've poisoned their minds, souls, and bodies; getting them to kill and eat the flesh of my animals;

Satan: Oh, my Lucifer, wait until they kill them all; your human race will become human cannibals.

God: Some battles of Good and evil you may have won; you will never win this WAR;

Satan: Are you sure? We shall see what the future has in store.

Heels, Dollars, and Life (*Date unknown*)

Her eyes on the mirror, looking at her face;

She's on a paper chase, more like a paper race.

Putting on her makeup; fixing up her hair;

She steps outside the dressing room, but her mind says, "don't you dare!"

She goes out; surrounded by wolves, pigs, and trolls;

She feels like Jesus being crucified; instead of the cross, she's hanging from poles.

All eyes on her, like a professor in a class;

What's going through her mind; while they're grabbing and smacking her ass.

Familiar dollars coming from stranger's hands,

The whispers of doom in her ears; offers requested for one-night stands.

Pulling her by her wrist, "let me get a dance;"

Not her cup of tea, but her job requires she takes that chance.

Dead presidential grass blankets the dance floor,

Dancing in those high heels all night, her feet are swollen and sore.

More & more liquor, Henny running through her bloodstreams;

A private dance; living her nightmares, while he's living his dreams.

Many nights intoxicated; her body's num, can't feel a thing;

All night long, her ass is smacked, it no longer stings.

End of the night, the heels are off; she's counting that money;

She wants out but needs in, bills and babies are no joke; no freebies honey.

A lot on her mind, but her family don't want to hear what she has to say;

Judging her like there's no tomorrow, she's only human at the end of the day.

She cried many tears, but always wiped them away;

The hell what her family thinks or what anyone has to say.

Looking in the mirror again, just asking herself, "how?"

Tupac said, "*protect your essence, you are still precious, smile for me now*."

April to October *(2/18/20)*

Her mother she loves; her mother the dancer,

A kiss to her hairless skull, momma is battling with cancer.

Her momma's number one fan, seeing her momma's beautiful dance,

Holding her hand, kissing her arm, this is her only chance.

"Dance with me baby, come dance with your mother,"

You're only blessed one mother on this earth; after that, there's no other.

Momma used to lift her to the sky,

Spread her arms like wings and pretended to fly,

Daughter now picks up momma, falling from weakening legs, momma crying, "I don't want to die."

Daughter lays in bed with momma, humming their favorite song,

A bond that is so strong, but soon won't be for long.

A daughter, not yet crossed the finish line of pre-teen years,

She remembers her momma on that stage, standing ovations, clapping hands, and all the cheers.

"My darling April," her momma begins to talk,

"The leaves are falling, please oh please can we go for a walk?"

"Momma you're too weak, I can't carry you, I'm just a little girl,"

“But I want to dance one last time, in the autumn leaves; just one last twirl.”

"I'll dance for you, momma; I'll dance while you're in bed."

"Okay baby, dance as the little angel you are, you are beautiful as I always said."

Humming their favorite song again; April dances and twirls, a little girl at play,

Disconnected duet; momma’s voice peacefully fades away.

April screams her favorite word, three commas:

“MOMMA, MOMMA, MOMMA, MOMMAAAAA!!!!!

References

1. *The Great Hack*. (2019). [film] Directed by K. Amer and J. Noujaim. New York City, England, UK, Thailand, Black Rock City, Nevada, USA: Netflix.

2. Lanier, J. (2018). *Ten Arguments for Deleting Your Social Media Accounts Right Now*. 1st ed. New York: Henry Holt and Company.

3. *When You're Strange*. (2009). [film] Directed by T. DiCillo.

4. Blake, W. (n.d.). *The Marriage of Heaven and Hell*.

5. Forster, E. and Forster, E. (n.d.). *The machine stops and other stories*.

6. *The View*, (2018). [TV programme] ABC: ABC.

7. Black-face.com. (2019). *Blackface! - The History of Racist Blackface Stereotypes*. [online] Available at: http://black-face.com [Accessed 17 Dec. 2019].

8. *Editors, H. (2009, November 9). Ronald Reagan. HISTORY. https://www.history.com/topics/us-presidents/ronald-reagan*
9. *The Jeffersonian Republicans and the Original Republican Party. (2017, March 31). ThoughtCo. https://www.thoughtco.com/democratic-republican-party-4135452*
10. *Editors, H. (2020, January 23). World War I. HISTORY. https://www.history.com/topics/world-war-i/world-war-i-history*
11. *World War II*. (n.d.). HISTORY. https://www.history.com/topics/world-war-ii